BREAKING
MIDNIGHT

A TRUE STORY

LYNN WALKER

MZW
PUBLISHING
Seattle WA
USA

Print ISBN: 978-1-7378955-4-1
eBook ISBN: 978-1-7378955-5-8

MZW Publishing
Washington USA
www.MZWPublishing.com

For Dad. Yeah, we did pretty good.

I've got my ticket for the long way 'round
Two bottles of whiskey for the way
And I sure would like some sweet company
Oh I'm leaving tomorrow, what d'ya say?

From "Cups (You're Gonna Miss Me)" by Luisa Gerstein

PREFACE BY THE AUTHOR

This is my father's story, which I wrote based on lengthy, recorded interviews I conducted with him over several years. Except for the prologue and epilogue that are told from my perspective, the entire story is written from his point of view, using his words and staying true to his voice. In some cases, dialogue was recreated to reflect Dad's recall about what was said. Also, in some instances, accurate, historic details were added to create a consistent, flowing narrative. To my knowledge, all of my father's recollections are true and, where possible, I corroborated his memories with court records, newspaper articles and interviews with others involved. While my father is no longer living, he reviewed a draft of this book, provided additional information and context, as needed, and wanted it to be published. At the request of my father, all of the names and some identifying details were changed to protect the privacy of individuals involved.

PROLOGUE: QUESTIONS

As soon as I hear Dad's voice, my body tenses. "What's wrong?" I ask.

"Nothin's wrong. Just wanna talk … can't a dad call his daughter just to talk?"

Sure you can, I think, but you never do. "Yeah. Of course. Glad you're okay."

He starts in with the small talk—how's my job, how do I like married life, how's our new house—then comes that long, heavy pause. I hate the emptiness between us. I run groups for teens whose parents are drug addicts and alcoholics, yet I can't narrow the gulf that exists between my father and me.

Just ask him something, something real, about his life. This is your chance. Ask him anything. "Hey Dad, I've been thinking for a few years now"—*more like a few decades*—"that I'd like to … um … hear your story. About what happened to you." My heart thumps in my chest as I press the phone to my ear. We rarely talk about the years Dad dished out his unlimited, uncut Colombian cocaine to my brother, Rick, and me until it nearly killed all three of us.

"What for? You think it'd be educational? Interesting?"

"Hah! Well, you have led a life not a lot people have. That would be interesting. But I just want to know what happened, about how you went from being an undercover narcotics agent to smuggling drugs."

The phone line hums. The laughter and squeals of neighborhood kids stream through my window. Soon, I hope to have children of my own who will be romping and playing outside, as carefree as I was in my early childhood. And no matter what, *I* will never slip out of the house in the dark of night, like my father did, and walk away from *my* kids.

"What do you wanna do, Lynn? Fly out here and interview me or somethin'?" He lets out a chuckle, a nervous-sounding one. I can't even fathom my dad being nervous, since I've seen him nervous exactly once in my life.

"Yeah, I can come out there. How about next month?" More phone silence. Uh-oh, I think. That was too pushy.

"Well, come on then."

When I arrive at Dad's house, we grapple for something to say to each other. I'm anxious to start the interview, to have a focus for our conversation. Mostly I'm worried I'll be too chickenshit to ask the questions that have been burning inside me for decades. Long ago, I gave up the fantasy he would ever try to be a father to me again, but I never gave up my fascination with his life.

How *did* a Miami undercover narcotics agent end up in prison for smuggling 12,000 pounds of marijuana—a Convair 440 airplane full? Perhaps a lot of Miami narcs became corrupt in the 1970s. Maybe Dad growing up as the son of a preacher had something to do with him becoming a convicted felon—a perfect rejection of his fundamentalist upbringing. But what happened to all my father's pride about being a Marine and a policeman? And wasn't he scared shitless when he started smuggling again—while on parole? This time, bringing in pure cocaine direct from Colombia.

Then the really hard questions. Why did he walk out on our family in the middle of the night, never to return? Yes, I know all about the sexy stewardess who became my first stepmother, but I didn't think anything was wrong with Mom, Rick and me. And how the hell did he justify dishing out cocaine to me and pulling Rick into his smuggling operations? Does he know that coke brought Rick and me to our knees? That Rick ended up in the ER with convulsions after smoking cocaine day after day without any food or sleep? How I became obsessed with that dense, crusty powder? How my mouth watered at the sight of the cocaine's pale pink chunks, flaky and glinting? Does he know that I became enslaved to his cocaine? Right up until four thirty a.m., when I crawled out of my attic where I'd hunkered off and on for days, alone, snorting coke from a bulging gallon Ziploc bag that I was hiding from the cops who were supposedly watching Rick's house?

Dad should know how his cocaine practically destroyed his kids' lives.

If I do find the courage to ask all my questions, I doubt

he'll answer them. I don't think he can. Not truthfully, anyways. But this is my chance. Maybe the only chance I'll ever get.

Subtly, I slide a tape recorder onto the coffee table—I purchased it just for these interviews, because I don't dare miss a single word. Something honest might slip out of his mouth. "You okay if I record this?"

Dad sits in a loveseat on the other side of the table, one long leg draped over the other, gently rocking his foot. At sixty, he still commands a room, his face open and ready for whatever comes his way, his smile disarming, his eyes mischievous. His hair and mustache are mostly still milk-chocolate-colored, now with a smattering of gray. He's strapping, even with a slight paunch, because at six feet tall, he carries that extra weight well. No doubt, women are still drawn to him. *I'm* still drawn to him, still captivated by the playful dad who taught me to deep-sea fish and sail the Keys and shoot targets with his gun, bull's-eye, all before I was seven. That father must be in there somewhere. Mom always said he was life-of-the-party funny, playful, a romantic. She also said that, by the time they were divorced, he was barreling through people's lives without any remorse for how he affected others.

He points at the tape recorder that looms between us. "That's fine, I guess." Scooching back into the couch, I try to relax. He purses his lips for a few seconds "But I'll probably want some prompts to focus my thoughts. You know … some questions."

A smile tugs at the corners of my mouth. "No problem there, Dad. I've got tons of questions."

I reach over and push the "Record" button.

CHAPTER 1
MISSING PERSON

I t was August 1968. Sweltering. The kind of heat that blankets Miami, settles over top of people, making it hard to breathe, making people crazy. I was wearing a riot helmet with a shield, sweat pouring down my face and neck, my chest and back. A hundred of us deputies blocked the road, forming a wall around the rioters, trying to stop them from trashing Liberty City. It was the second riot there that summer, though we got calls about murders and robberies in that neighborhood of Miami every day.

With a few hundred people all crammed together, everyone got hotter and angrier, including us cops. The rioters raised their fists in the air and shouted in our faces: "Black Power!" and "Get out of here, you motha fuckin' crackers." I was lit up with adrenaline. If someone charged at me, I swung my billy club—left, right, behind me, out front, wherever they were coming from. We were trained not to let rioters get close enough to get a hold of you or your gun, so I wasn't about to let either happen. If that happens, it's all over, because police are always outnumbered in a riot.

Eventually, the National Guard trucks rolled in and sprayed tear gas into the crowd. Then one of those torrential downpours started. That broke things up. Seemed like the temperature dropped ten degrees just getting them out of our faces.

Next morning, I was showing my kids, Lynn and Rick, my riot gear, and our dog went berserk barking at me. With that big, shielded helmet, I probably looked like an alien to her. While the kids were cracking up, I noticed the inside of my helmet was still damp with sweat and stunk like smoke and bitter tear gas. That's when it crossed my mind I could've gotten hurt at the riot. A few people had been killed—no cops—but that was a risk I hadn't even considered. I was a rookie and, a few years earlier, had been an MP in the Marine Corps. And I grew up obeying very religious parents (least they thought I was). So I knew how to take orders. I followed directions, went where the captain sent me, did what I was told to do. Guess that's why it was easy to walk into dangerous situations and keep my head; I just didn't think about getting hurt. I knew I might shoot some criminal, but I'd be fine.

I loved police work. When I was after someone, my adrenaline would be pumping. I may not have known who they were or what they did, but I'd catch them if I had to run them off the highway to do it. There's nothing like the thrill of a chase, so exciting and energizing.

Course, some of the work was gross, like the time I checked on a car pulled off the side of the road. This lady was in there in labor, couldn't get to the hospital in time.

Blood and shit and fluid was all over the seat. Said she could feel the baby's head. Whoa, I did *not* need to hear that. I called an ambulance and stayed by her car, reassuring her an ambulance was on the way. There wasn't anything more I could do. I didn't know how to deliver a damn baby. Just kept telling her it'd be there any minute— the ambulance not the baby, I was thinking—and kept my sights off the mess underneath her.

Missing-persons cases were the worst. You never knew what would come from those, usually nothing good. Approaching the mobile home of a missing man once, the stench from that trailer told me he was dead already, probably had been for days. *Nothing* smells worse than a putrid, decomposing body. And in a trailer. In the Miami heat. Instantly, I began to breathe through my mouth and made an about-face to return to the cruiser.

My partner Tina—only female partner I ever had, and she was good, didn't take shit from anyone—was just walking up to the trailer. "I take it you found him in there?"

My stomach was twisted up with nausea, but luckily I didn't start gagging. Wouldn't that be impressive, retching and throwing up right on the sidewalk at her feet. "Oh, he's in there alright. I don't gotta see him, I can smell him."

"Great. I'll go call it in."

"I'm gonna get something from the trunk to cover my nose and mouth before I go in there."

She stuck her head out of the cruiser while I was rifling through the trunk. "John, get something for my face too, will ya?"

Luckily, for me and Tina (not for the missing man), it looked like a homicide case. We turned that nasty scene over to the homicide detectives and got the hell out of that trailer.

That's around the time I started teaching my wife, Linda, and the kids how to handle and shoot my guns.

The one case I'll never forget as long as I live was a little girl who'd gone missing. She was about four and had been gone about an hour when we got to the girl's house. My partner then, Jerry—a big-ass man, little overweight but mostly bulky and tall, even had a few inches on me, like six-foot-five—searched the house for any sign of anything suspicious, while I questioned the parents about when they last saw her, where they searched so far. Hard-ass as it sounds, we were looking for signs of any funny business. There are some sick parents out there, and we needed to assess whether this could be a homicide case.

Jerry came back into the kitchen, shrugged at me. Wasn't anything suspicious on my end either. Lynn kept popping into my thoughts because she was about the same age as that missing girl. I was trying to think of what a little girl would do if she wandered out of the house, though Lynn knew better than to do that. Our house rule was that the kids told us if they were going outside and where. Always. And our pool was off-limits to our kids unless me or Linda were on the patio with them. But that's always where they wanted to go: swimming.

Jerry and I stepped into the living room where the parents couldn't hear us. "You check the pool?" I asked.

"Yeah. Didn't see anything. I'll take the father and ask the neighbors if they've seen her."

"I'll take the mother and drive around, make a two-mile radius. That's about as far as she could get on foot by now."

Jerry tucked his chin down to his chest and said quietly, "Unless someone's snatched her." He looked back up at me.

I nodded. We were both thinking it. When you've seen enough of these cases, that's where your mind goes: to the worst-case scenario. You want to save a life, start with the most dire, most dangerous possibilities and rule those out first. Then work your way down to the less urgent scenarios.

As I drove the streets, the mother called out the girl's name with a bullhorn then listened for her daughter responding, for any sound of her calling out for her mama. Kids in danger always want their mamas. Forty minutes later, we returned to the house empty-handed. I checked in with Jerry. None of the neighbors had seen her or anything suspicious.

Something kept nagging at me to scan the pool one more time. Unbeknownst to me and Jerry, the parents had treated the pool with chemicals late that morning. The water, still milky from the chemicals, was just starting to clear. As soon as I got to the patio door, I saw a small, cloudy, dark shape at the bottom of the deep end. A current, like electricity, shot into my arms and legs, and I crashed through the screen door and dove into the water.

When I pulled her tiny body out, I knew she was dead. Her body was stiff. I couldn't stand there and do nothing, so I tried to resuscitate her. Her lips were the palest shade of blue and so very, very cold. Her lungs were full of water. I couldn't blow even a tiny bit of air into her lungs.

Right next to my head, the mother was bouncing from one foot to the other, screaming, "No! No! No! Oh, God, please, please." Jerry finally pulled me off the girl, the parents collapsing over her body while we radioed for a coroner.

When I got home that night, I didn't take off my holster or my uniform or lock up my gun before I went to check on Lynn and Rick. As I stared at them, I was brutally aware how impossible it would be to protect them from everything the world was going to throw at them. There was so much danger out there, so many whackos.

Didn't sleep much that night. Every time I closed my eyes, I saw that little girl's blue lips.

Uniformed duty was like that, you had to deal with whatever came your way: riots, blood, gore … dead children. Cases like that little missing girl made me start to dislike uniformed duty.

Luckily, the director of the Organized Crime Bureau recruited me during my second year with Dade County Public Safety Department. They were desperate for more detectives to work narcotics, so I agreed to give it a shot.

Undercover, I got another car, an apartment, sometimes even an undercover girlfriend. Have to admit, that was always fun: only legit way a married man can have a girlfriend on the side. Agents could also drink and use drugs in the line of duty. Had to, because that's what drug dealers do. You can't go in to score drugs all straitlaced and refusing hits and drinks. Our work was done on the streets, in bars and hotels, sometimes dealers' houses or our undercover apartments.

Each night, I drove varied, convoluted routes to stop and switch back to my personal vehicle. Then I took the long way home and made sure I wasn't followed. I was forever checking my rearview mirror.

Narcotics agents didn't have much supervision. Occasionally, I went to a covert location to meet with other agents or my supervisor, because I couldn't walk in the front door of the police station. We weren't clocking in and out every day either. We went out, built connections with informants and dealers, worked our way up to the sources and took out the smuggling rings. We had a lot of leeway, and I took it. Took all of it.

I loved the narcotics work right away. Was good at it too: nurturing relationships with drug dealers—a long, slow building of trust to convince a dealer I was one of them. The other detectives who trained me said I was a natural. Probably got that from my father. He could put a congregation at ease right away, church members warming to him from the get-go. People gravitated towards my father, they opened up, told him their problems. Not just at church either. Pop was always ministering to folks: over the phone, in our living room, during Sunday dinners. I always wanted to have that same way with people and assumed Pop's ability to disarm people came from being a preacher. Until I started working narcotics. Then I realized that disarming people was a skill I could develop and hone. I perfected that skill as a narc, could snow anyone, make them believe whatever I wanted them to believe.

Turned out I was a good businessman too, buying and selling drugs, making deals. And drug smuggling was serious business in Miami.

As an undercover agent, I had to think, act, talk and live like a drug dealer. When I walked out of our house each day, I left that family man behind, the man who took his family to church every Sunday, and I became a drug dealer.

My first and only undercover partner was Carl—best partner anyone could ask for. He was several years younger than me, in his early twenties, and new to the force. A lanky, good-looking kid and sharp, a real fast learner. It can take a while to know, without a doubt, that you can rely on a partner, but we were tight from the beginning, had instant chemistry. You need that when you're working undercover, because you have to come off like you're buddies, or at least like you regularly sell and buy drugs to and from each other. There has to be a natural flow between you, or your cover is blown. Drug dealers have radar for any inconsistencies between what you and your partner say or any fumbling for answers, shit like that, but Carl and I were seamless. We trusted each other with our lives. We had to.

CHAPTER 2
A GOOD DAY

Undercover cases could last for months, even years. One case we worked on for several months started when a uniformed officer stopped a young woman whose car had been swerving in and out of lanes. She had a baby in the car and was clearly high. The officer suspected drugs since she didn't reek like alcohol. He searched her car and found a handgun under the seat along with a small baggie of what the lab confirmed was heroin. The narcotics department was contacted in case the arrest led to something bigger. Carl and I were assigned to the case.

We questioned this lady, Melanie, about where she'd been getting her heroin. She wouldn't talk. Just sat there with her shoulders slumped over, staring at the table in front of her. Once we questioned her ability to take care of her baby, she started blubbering about how she was trying, really trying, to get off the heroin, signed up at a methadone clinic and on and on. That's what all the junkies said, that they were kicking the habit. Heard it all before.

"Just tell us where you're gettin' it," Carl said. "And we'll tell Child Protective Services you're cooperating. That you're tryin' to straighten up for your baby."

She finally looked at us, all puffy-eyed and snotty. "Promise? I can get my baby back?"

We had no idea if CPS would let her have the baby back, depended on how bad things were at her home. We both nodded.

She wiped the tears off her face and ran the back of her hand under her nose, cleared her throat. "I get it from my baby's father."

"Name?" I asked.

"David."

"David what?"

"Remos. David Remos."

"Where is he?" Carl asked.

She shrugged. "Gone for work right now. He rebuilds used auto parts then sells them. In Mexico."

Carl and I looked at each other. We were on to something because most of the heroin in Miami came from Mexico.

"He'll be home this weekend."

There were no warrants for David Remos, so we couldn't take him into custody. We alerted officials in Texas to search David's vehicle if he came through customs. He never came through, least not with that name. I'm sure Melanie told him she'd been arrested, warned him that we had his name.

For weeks, we watched the couple's apartment but never saw David. We asked around the streets to see if anyone knew David and where he was, said we were looking to buy some of that good smack we'd heard about. No one had seen him in weeks. He was keeping a low profile. We even roughed up one of our informants, this small-time heroin dealer who'd been arrested a few months earlier, to get him to talk. We invited him to go for a ride with us then took him out to the Everglades. Don't know why—guess we were hungry—but we stopped on the way and got a bucket of fried chicken. For an hour we harassed that poor man, waving our guns around, threatening him, all the while laughing and eating our Kentucky Fried Chicken.

"You know," I said, "a body could disappear out here in the Glades. Gators probably eat all the evidence overnight."

"C'mon, man. Why you harassin' me? I ain't done a thing to you guys. I told you a million times, I ain't seen David for months. Why would I lie? Why don't y'all leave me alone?"

We got sick of his pleading and begging and were sure he didn't have any info, so we gave him the rest of our chicken and left him alone alright. On the side of road, Alligator Alley, next to one of those road signs that warn people to stay in their cars.

"Hope he hitches a ride soon," Carl said.

"He will. That's a busy highway. And if he doesn't, he can always throw that chicken to the gators, so they'll leave him alone." We chuckled and drove away.

A few weeks later, I was driving my family to church and took a small detour by David's apartment. There it was, his car, right out front. I pulled over near an old barn, jumped out and told Linda to go on to church but to stop and call Carl from the first pay phone she saw. "Just tell him the guy we been lookin' for is at his apartment. Tell him to get over here and pick me up at the barn down the street from the guy's place. Tell him to hurry." Lynn and Rick were staring at me with their mouths hanging open, probably wondering why I was skipping out on church. Rick wanted to know if I was after a bad guy; it was all a game to him, cops-and-robbers stuff.

Carl and I followed David to a motel that had several individual units, like little cabins, and staked it out all day and into the night. This was too big to let other detectives take over the surveillance. Late that first night, we sat in our unmarked car, smoked and talked about everything: our families, basketball, women, our lieutenant, the sheriff. Part of the time we just stared out the window, waiting, watching. Eventually, we took turns snoozing.

After a day of watching David, and lots of other people coming and going to his unit, we were sure he was in there dealing. With our surveillance and the information Melanie had provided, we were able to get a warrant the next morning to put wireless bugs in his motel room.

When David finally left early that afternoon, we got the keys from the desk clerk and placed bugs under two table lamps. We settled into an adjacent cabin where transmission to our receiver would be the clearest, and we had line of sight to the door of his room. For a second evening, we listened to him dealing heroin in his room, providing enough evidence to arrest him or at least coerce him into telling us who his supplier was.

As it was getting dark, Melanie showed up with their baby. I looked at Carl and shook my head. The last thing we wanted to do was bust into that room, guns drawn, with a kid in there. We listened to her talking incessantly to David —the frantic talk of a junkie in withdrawal. We heard her shooting up, then her speech got all drawn-out and slurred. Then we heard the silence of a junkie who just got a big hit. All the while, her daughter was babbling happily in the background. Disgust and fury washed over Carl's face, mirroring exactly how I felt.

Eventually, our receiver crackled with the silence from their room. We discussed our options and decided to enter their room before dawn, when they'd still be asleep, groggy from the heroin and the least likely to resist arrest or flee. And the baby would be sleeping, better than being in Melanie's arms. Then we took turns getting a couple of hours of sleep.

Early the next morning, before the sky had started to lighten, we crept along the front of their unit with our guns drawn. My body was tight with tension and I was glad, because it removed any weariness I'd been feeling.

Carl pounded on the door and shouted, "Dade County Sheriff, open up!" My gun was aimed chest-high at the edge of the door where it'd open.

From inside came scrambling noises and whispering, then baby screams. That threw me off for a split second, because if things went sideways and they started shooting at us, we didn't want gunfire with a baby around. Hard to imagine parents firing a gun around a baby, but can't rule anything out in a drug scene like that. Carl and I made eye contact. No turning back now though. I ticked my chin at the door. Carl pounded again. "Open up!"

As we heard the door being unlatched, I shoved it open. "Hands up! Both of you, now. Up, up!"

"What the fuck is going on? You can't barge in here like this," David yelled, but he kept his arms in the air. Good, no resistance.

Carl waved the search warrant at them and dropped it on the table, moved to the bathroom, back against the wall, gun out in front. "Clear back here," he called out. Their little girl was wailing by then, and Melanie moved towards her.

I pointed my gun at her. "Don't move. Stay right there." I opened the drawer of the nightstand and pulled out a .38 revolver, dumped the bullets out and shoved them in my pocket.

Carl grabbed David's arm and twisted it hard and close behind his back. "We're just gonna talk right now. We're not arresting you."

"Yet," I added.

"We just wanna talk," he said, "but we don't want any fuckin' funny business. Got it?"

David nodded.

Looking at Melanie, I jerked my head at the baby and said, "See if you can calm her down."

While David pulled some pants on, I surveyed the room and found a few syringes stuffed under the mattress. When I dropped the syringes onto the table, I could see the craving in their eyes. Carl found a bag of heroin, probably a hundred grams or so, stuffed inside a slit in one of the pillows. He tossed it from hand to hand, watching Melanie stare at it. She looked even worse than when we'd questioned her a couple of months earlier. David's hair was matted and tangled, and dark circles hung under his eyes.

We interrogated David all morning, but he wouldn't tell

us where he got his heroin. The room was hot and stale and reeked of overflowing ashtrays and dirty diapers, but we left the air conditioner off. The air pressed down on us until I felt like smacking David around. The baby cowered in Melanie's lap, while Melanie picked at sores on her arms and constantly bounced her leg up and down, either trying to comfort the baby or agitated from coming down off the heroin. I couldn't tell which.

Later that morning, Child Protective Services got there to take custody of the baby, who was still whimpering, scared and starving, I'm sure.

"David, tell them what they want," Melanie screamed. Shit, we had to hold her back while CPS left with the wailing baby. The baby was reaching over the social worker's shoulder, grasping and clutching for her mother. That really pissed me off, that they could do this to that poor little thing, bring her into this drug world, shoot up in front of her, risk her life even. These weren't the leaders of this heroin ring, just a couple of junkies trying to hold their shit together to do some dealing. Anyone who was very successful at dealing heroin didn't use it.

As soon as the social workers left, Melanie collapsed onto the bed, sobbing. We slapped David around a little, but he still wouldn't talk.

Carl pointed over his shoulder with his thumb. "Look at what you're doin' to your family, man."

Melanie sat up and yelled. "Fucking tell them. Just fucking tell them."

His shirt was drenched with sweat and his hands were trembling. "If I talk"—he looked from Melanie to me to Carl —"if I tell you, then we get our baby back?"

"CPS'll work with you if you talk, but you gotta get off this junk." I pointed to the syringes and the bag of heroin. He looked at Melanie again.

Melanie glared at David, pleading all over her face. "Please get my baby back. *Please*."

"Will I go to jail?" he asked.

"Not if you talk," Carl said.

An informant with David's connection—someone he was getting virtually uncut heroin from—would be a big win for us. A big part of undercover work is flipping a suspect into an informant. Turning someone into a good informant wasn't easy, because you're basically asking them to become a rat. Nobody likes a rat. So an informant had to have a lot more to lose by keeping their mouth shut than by informing. Always a lousy choice, but it worked out good for us agents. Agents made lots of promises to informants—some we could deliver on, some we couldn't—to get them to that tipping point.

We were betting that David's tipping point was their baby; she gave David a lot to lose if he didn't start talking. For that reason, it was a good thing they had a baby. And for that reason alone, because that little girl was going to have a shit life with those parents.

Carl and I waited in silence, watching David.

Finally, he began to spill his guts. He told us his main supplier was a guy went by the name of Hector. Hell no, he said, he didn't know his last name. David described where they crossed the border in Texas and described how they used cargo trucks with false walls to hide the heroin, and how they paid hitchhikers to drive the trucks into Miami. He told us when the next load was expected to arrive in

Miami and agreed to introduce us to Hector—*if* we helped them get their baby back.

"Like we said, we'll talk to CPS," I said.

While we waited for the next load of heroin to come in, we talked, undercover, with a couple of smaller heroin dealers around the city, the guys selling thirty-dollar bags that were, at best, 25 percent heroin. Said we wanted some of this really good smack we'd been hearing about and were willing to pay good money for it. Word on the street was the only person you could get that good shit from was David. His heroin was apparently so good, that no one else could sell their heroin for a decent price when David's stuff was available. So, when David came into town with heroin, other dealers simply pulled their lower-quality stuff off the streets until David sold all of his.

We were definitely onto a main Mexican supplier, Hector, because the stuff we'd confiscated from David tested at 75 percent pure heroin. We'd never seen heroin of that quality on the streets before.

When the next load arrived, David had us come to his apartment and introduced us to Hector. Because David vouched for us, Hector agreed to sell us a small amount of heroin, twenty-five grams, though he was skittish about that. No one likes to sell to a stranger, in case they're a cop. But we were gambling that Hector trusted David.

We knew there was way more than an ounce at stake, so Carl said, "Ah man, we need more than that. We can move that in a day."

Hector nodded, pensively. "Bueno. You come back mañana … then maybe I sell you more."

Carl acted cool. "Alright. We can dig it. We'll be back in the mornin'."

We had the lab test the heroin—the sample came back almost 100 percent heroin. No wonder Hector's stuff was so good; it was almost pure heroin. That meant he was no middleman; he was the smuggler. He was bringing it into the U.S. uncut and probably in large quantities. We had to nail him, but we needed him to hand over a larger amount of heroin to make a big bust.

We went back the next day, and I gave him $10,000 in cash. Cash in hand was the best way to solidify a deal. "Man, your stuff's the best. We need more right away, cuz it's gone already."

He fondled a stack of the bills, counted how many hundreds were in it, looked back and forth between David, me and Carl. He held a few hundred-dollar bills up to the ceiling light and checked both sides of each bill. For a second, I thought David had ratted us out. Stay cool, I told myself, stay cool.

Carl lifted his hands in the air. "Well? There's your money. Where's our smack?"

"Cuanto?" Hector asked.

"Half a kilo," I said.

"Sí. But I go get it first." This is exactly what we wanted him to do, so we could bust him with what we hoped was a large quantity.

"Man, we're not gonna sit here and wait. When'll you have it? We'll come back," Carl said.

"Una hora. Aqui." He pointed at the floor. "Be here in one hour."

We all shook hands on the deal and Carl and I left David's apartment first.

Backup was all around the apartment complex, but they hung back unless they heard or saw something go sideways. If all went as planned, backup would then follow our car.

We tailed Hector to a big house in the woods. As we snuck around the back of the house, we could see through the pine trees that he was in his backyard, dirty and sweaty, digging up bags of heroin.

We signaled for the deputies to move in. As soon as Hector saw them, he shot at the police, then bolted into the woods. As we heard the story later, they chased him through the woods and into a nearby park, with a bunch of kids running around. Can't shoot at a fleeing suspect in that environment. They had K-9 units and a helicopter searching for Hector, but they never caught him. We never heard about him or saw him again; probably went back to Mexico. But we did dig up eight pounds of *uncut* heroin from Hector's yard that day. At the time, that heroin bust was the largest in Miami's history.

Man, that was a good day.

CHAPTER 3
GOING HOME

The narcotics work made me feel invincible and so alive, despite the danger, or probably because of it. Some cases were risker than others, but Carl and I always had each other's backs.

During surveillance on one smuggling ring, we heard two dealers talking over their tapped phone lines about trying to eliminate the "new guy"—me. Didn't sound like they figured out I was a narc. We would've pulled the plug on the operation right away if they had. I was just a new man, who they didn't know or trust, brought into the group by Leo. I'd been building a relationship with him for months after learning that he could get hundreds of bales of marijuana from a person he described only as "a Cuban smuggler."

This is what we wanted, to work our way up to the people running the smuggling rings, the ones bringing in boatloads of drugs. At that time, many of those people were Cubans, bringing marijuana, cocaine and heroin from South America or Mexico on boats, traveling through Cuba,

Bahamas, the Keys and into Southern Florida for distribution.

Leo was trying to pull the money together for at least eighty bales, so he invited me into the deal if I could contribute $25,000. From the conversation we heard over the wire, Leo's partners didn't have anything to lose by eliminating me once they got my share of the money. They stood to make another $100,000 each that way. Their scheme was to wait until I delivered my $25,000, whack me, go get the marijuana and split my twenty bales between them.

To keep me safe, the plan was that I'd insist on making the money exchange somewhere public: no hotel room or remote area. Then the arrest would be made by uniformed officers, without me present, when Leo and his guys went to get the drugs from the Cuban.

When Leo called me at my undercover apartment to say the boat was due the next night, I acted all excited that the deal was finally happening.

"Alright. Now we're talkin'. Meet you at the Last Chance bar with my share around nine tomorrow night." The Last Chance was a seedy little bar named that because it was the last bar heading south on Highway 1 before driving into the Keys. Not much but Everglades between The Last Chance and the Keys, twenty miles of it on either side of a straight, flat road. The saloon had no windows and only a couple doors, and no other buildings around it. A good place for smuggling activities. And that made The Last Chance a great place for undercover work.

"Nah man, not there," Leo said. I looked at Carl and shook my head.

Carl motioned for me to keep talking, rolling his fingers in a forward direction.

"What's the problem? Do it all the time. Come in. Have a drink. I'll set my briefcase down. Few minutes later, you walk out with it. Bada-bing, we're done." That was true, we did do it all the time. Carl and I bought a lot of drugs at the Last Chance.

"No way. Too public. How 'bout I come to your place?"

"Too public? What d'you mean? It'll be packed at nine o'clock. No one'll notice a thing. That's where I'll be. Nine tomorrow night." I hung up and let out a long exhale. "He didn't like it."

"He'll be there. They need the money," Carl said. "They can't go to the man twenty-five thousand short. He'll show."

We made sure to have plenty of backup that night. Three unmarked cop cars were stationed around the bar. The only way out was past one of the unmarked vehicles, which would then tail Leo or his partners to the boat. Once the money left the bar, it'd lead us to the boat, to the drugs. Without the drugs, we had nothing.

Carl was in the bar an hour before I got there, and both of us wore mics so the agents outside could hear every word that was said. Fifteen minutes after nine, I strolled into the bar with a thin black briefcase full of money. I scanned the bar. Leo and one of his guys was there, each sitting alone at different tables. The third guy was to meet them at the boat with a cargo truck to load the bales into. Good, everything was proceeding as planned.

I set the briefcase at the foot of my stool and ordered a double scotch, neat. I was grateful for the pungency and the warm burn of the scotch in my throat. That was probably my fourth drink of the day, so I was cool and calm, feeling in control. Reflected in the mirror behind the rows of booze bottles, I watched Leo walking towards the bar. He sat down next to me and ordered Jack on the rocks. I drank my scotch, watching the room behind me in the mirror. After several minutes, Leo paid the bartender, picked up the briefcase and walked out the front door.

Carl coughed twice, his signal to the agents outside that the money was exiting the building. Within a few minutes, Leo's partner left. Carl followed shortly thereafter.

It was all in the hands of Carl and the other officers now. They'd tail Leo to the supplier, to the boat, and make the arrest. If the boat was moored somewhere in Biscayne Bay, the arrest wouldn't take long. If the drop was in the Keys, it could take all night. All I had to do now was sit tight and wait to hear from Carl.

Too wound up to leave, I lit a cigarette and sipped my second scotch. Then behind me I heard the distinct click of high-heeled shoes. Oh, that was a tantalizing sound. This sexy woman walked up beside me and said, "Can I sit here?"

I smiled, slid a chair out for her and motioned the bartender over.

By the time Carl came back to the bar a few hours later, I was pretty drunk and cozy with that woman in a back booth. She'd kicked off her shoe and was inching her bare foot up the inside of my leg. Carl walked all the way up to our table before I noticed him. Goes to show how off my game I was by then, focusing only on this woman and my next scotch. That was sloppy. No matter how many drinks I'd had, when I was undercover (and even when I wasn't), I needed to be aware of what was going on around me.

"Hey, Tom. How you doin'?" I said, using his undercover name. I never got so sloppy that I blew our covers. Looking at the woman, I said, "This is my friend … ah…"

Carl smiled and shook his head while I struggled to remember her name.

She glared at me for a second, then extended her hand to Carl. "April. My name's April."

Carl shook her hand and said, "I'm Tom. Good to meet you." Motioning for me to follow him, he said, "I could use some advice. You got a minute?"

"Sure. Well, April, it was nice meetin' you."

She scribbled on a napkin and slid it to me. "Here's my number."

I stood and tucked the napkin in my pocket. "I'm movin' to a new apartment this weekend. No phone number yet. Maybe I'll see you in here another time."

She rolled her eyes and slid out of the booth.

Carl and I hurried out of the bar, and I scanned the parking lot before saying, "Well?"

"Nailed 'em all."

"How much'd we get?"

"Two hundred bales," he said, beaming.

We slapped high fives, and I let out a whoop. "Damn. You are the *kid*."

"You did pretty good yourself. Listen, I'm headin' home, man. It's late, and I'm beat. You goin' back in there?"

"In there?" I tipped my head back at the bar. "Nah. Was just killin' time in there."

Carl raised his eyebrows. "Killin' time? Is that what you call it now?"

I lifted my hands up, innocent. "I'm goin', I'm goin'. See you tomorrow."

Trying to live two lives, and keeping my two worlds separate, became more and more difficult. Whenever I went out with my family to public places like Matheson Hammock Park or down to the Keys to sail, I needed to be vigilant. I was ever-aware of the seedy otherworld all around us. Church or family places like the zoo were pretty safe bets, but I never knew where I might run into one of the hippies or druggies I worked with. On the few occasions when my two worlds did collide, I was frantic to protect my family and keep my real identity from the drug dealers. If I ran into someone who thought I was single and there I was with two kids and a wife, it'd blow my cover. All of us agents knew which dealers were nuts and would just as soon kill a narcotics agent as look at him. And if blowing my cover didn't get me killed, it'd prevent me from working undercover anymore. At least not in Miami; word spread fast about a narc.

I never took Linda or the kids to the area where my apartment was or to any of the neighborhoods or establishments we cruised down in Homestead, Kendall or south Miami. Those weren't places to take a family. They weren't as bad as the beats I'd been assigned to when I was in uniform, like the ghettos in Goulds where a war was underway between Blacks and Cubans, neither of which liked a "cracker" or "pig," as I was referred to daily when I worked there. The narcotics beats were nicer, but they still weren't the classiest parts of southern Florida.

Now, the smugglers running those drug rings, they lived in some nice places— mansions, dazzling pools, patios tiled in limestone, courtyards with huge fountains— in Miami Beach, Palm Beach, West Palm Beach. The wealth of these smugglers was unbelievable, excess in everything: clothes, cars, homes, women. I wouldn't have minded that lifestyle myself if I could've afforded it—much nicer than the one in my house in Cutler Ridge, with its dinky pool.

After a couple of years working undercover, Linda and I weren't getting along very well. Not sure if my work was just taking a toll on me or if our honeymoon phase was wearing off now that we'd been married for several years or both. She complained that I wasn't home enough and was always prodding and pushing me to talk to her. I *did* talk to her, told her about work all the time, even when dangerous stuff was going down because she wasn't bothered by much, wasn't a worrier or squeamish. Heck, she'd been an emergency-room nurse before our kids were born. Talk about seeing lots of blood and gore. But nothing fazed her. She used to watch surgeries from the observation room at the hospital while eating lunch. But it wasn't work she wanted me to talk about, she wanted me to talk about … I don't know what, feelings and crap. I couldn't explain how hard it was to be myself, my old self, when I was a drug dealer eight, ten, twelve hours a day. She wouldn't have understood. No one would've, except other agents. And we didn't talk about shit like that.

I began to dread going home, certain that something

really exciting would happen out on the streets the moment I went home. There were so many hopping nightclubs that I frequented, waiting for April or some other foxy distraction to show up. And they always did. This was during the disco scene, so bars were packed all night long with loud music, loose women, wealthy men and free-flowing cash, booze and drugs. I spent many a wild night at those bars, staying in my undercover role long after my shift was over. I would've never married one of those women from the nightclubs; they were just entertaining and fun to spend an evening with. My marriage and family still meant something to me, but it just couldn't hold my interest like before. Not as much as that intoxicating undercover life.

That underworld was getting harder and harder for me to separate myself from; that's where, and who, I wanted to be. Craved being part of that scene. Miami's underworld was calling to me, sucking me in. It was like an addiction, of sorts.

Compared to the intensity of my undercover life, home life couldn't stir much excitement in me anymore. Home was predictable, dull. It was the one place I could truly relax, there or out on a boat, but when I let my guard down and wasn't constantly calculating risk and assessing danger, I was completely drained. Impersonating a drug dealer day after day was exhausting. Even if I wasn't closing in on a bust, I was always amped up. As I was making deals, I was ready to react at any moment if our cover was blown or a drug exchange went bad or some dealer, whacked out on drugs, became paranoid or crazy. You don't feel the drain when you're working though, because you're in fight-or-flight mode. All day long.

I really liked the me that was undercover: a sly, smooth-talking, wheeling-and-dealing drug smuggler who people gravitated towards. A guy *women* gravitated towards. What can I say? I got married at nineteen—in 1962. Then the sexual revolution exploded: birth control pills and free love and Miami. Women were everywhere. Scantily clad women. They came into those nightclubs practically, and sometimes end up actually, topless. They were all over me. And I have to confess, I was all over them.

Every day, I flipped an internal switch on and off, on and off. Undercover agent—dad. Drug trafficker—church-goer. Charismatic, single, dealer—married man. On—off. On—off. Only I couldn't always find the damn switch right away. And some days, I didn't want to flip it off and come home.

After a few years, the narcotics work started getting really dangerous. When we bought and sold drugs with people on the streets, the dealers, it wasn't so bad. But once we started working our way up to some big-time smugglers, the people bringing the drugs into the country, they didn't care about killing us. The stakes were so high for them; they had millions of dollars—empires—to lose if they got busted.

In the early 1970s, the Cubans controlled most of the drugs that came into Miami, usually from South America and Mexico. But the Cubans didn't always make good on the deals, didn't always pay the drug lords back for all the drugs. Now, illegal or not, the Colombians take great pride in their work. They were disgusted with the way the Cubans ran their smuggling operations. Eventually, the Colombians under Pablo Escobar came into Miami and methodically eliminated the Cubans from the drug trafficking. When I started on the police force, Escobar was robbing cabs for a living. By the mid-70s, he was a multi-billionaire. Escobar's law was, "No more Cubans." Miami got bloody violent then. No more strutting into an undercover op without any thought about the danger.

Agents used whatever tools they could to take the edge off. For me, it was primarily drinking. Booze allowed me to push the danger to the back of my mind, to step out of myself, allowed me to *be* someone else. That's precisely what I needed. I couldn't be an undercover agent pretending to be a dealer, no matter how good I was. I needed to *be* a drug dealer. This was the beginning of what would become a long love affair with scotch. With my first taste of that smoky, rich scotch each day, I could feel myself relaxing. It sounds strange, since I always had such bad ulcers and stomach problems, but scotch actually settled my stomach. As soon as that first drink entered my bloodstream, I slipped right into my drug-smuggling self. That switch was flipped, and I was all the way on.

For the most part, I stayed off the drugs when I was undercover. The government had passed a law in 1971 that an undercover agent could use drugs in the line of duty. So, if we were working a cocaine deal, I always snorted lines. Always liked cocaine. Or toked on a joint when I had to, but pot made me paranoid. If we were working a heroin ring, I told dealers I was buying smack for my old lady, or said, "I'm allergic to that shit, man. I just sell it." That usually worked for me. Sometimes a drug dealer got suspicious, but the money was too good; they couldn't turn it down. No way was I shooting heroin into my veins. That kind of drug use, that's some bad business there. And the last thing an agent wants to do is get wasted on smack. You can't be nodding off, you got to be alert and vigilant.

After a few years of undercover work and some pretty heavy drinking, I stopped wanting to shed my identity as a drug dealer and go home to the suburbs. Every night, I went out after work for a few more drinks to unwind before going home. After a while, a few more drinks turned into several more, and, eventually, I didn't go home until the middle of the night, until I was drunk.

One morning I woke up with a head-throbbing hangover, and Linda started in after me. How she hated me coming home at all hours of the night and not being home enough and not spending time with the kids anymore. All true. I turned on the charm, trying to make her laugh, romancing her, nuzzling her ear. Worked in the past, but she wasn't falling for any of my maneuvers that morning.

She shrugged me off and said, "John, try being serious for one minute, will you? I'm worried about you. About us. Maybe you need to go back to uniform duty. This undercover work has changed you. You're like this ... completely different person."

I let out a big scoffing, "Hah!" That's exactly what my job required: for me to be a completely different person. Every day. And now I was being criticized for a skill that was highly difficult to achieve, potentially life-saving and one I was damn good at. But I was no dummy; I wasn't going to say any of that to her. Out of excuses and tactics, I flipped that switch and, poof, was gone. I was gone before I even left the house. "Let's talk about this later, okay? I gotta get to work. We got a—"

"Yeah, yeah. I know"—she threw her hand up, a giant stop sign for me to just save it—"a big case. You and Carl always have one. Just go work on your 'big case.' Go on."

"Drug smugglers don't work nine-to-five, know what I mean? This kind of work all happens late at night, darlin'. It's the nature of the business."

"I've got to get the kids up for school." She headed out of the kitchen.

"I'll try to get home earlier tonight. No guarantees," I said to her back. "Don't wait up."

She spun around, glaring at me. "Don't worry. I never do."

CHAPTER 4
LIVING TWO LIVES

I t was after midnight, and I was on my way home from a bar when a sheriff's car passed me with its lights on then turned into an apartment complex. In case the deputies needed any backup, I followed it. Turned out to be two airline stewardesses who appeared to have been out doing some drinking of their own and locked themselves out of their apartment. When the neighbor had heard some noises and whispering, and saw someone trying to get in the window, she called the cops. Both of the women were pretty—this was back in the day when stewardesses had to be attractive, and these two certainly were. Laura was a dark-haired beauty, a sweet-talking, Southern belle with large breasts and long legs. I wasn't wearing my wedding ring because I'd been undercover all day, and I was kind of glad I didn't have it on. Before I left, she invited me to a party at their apartment.

I shouldn't have gone to that party, but I couldn't get her sexy accent, or her breasts, out of my head all week. We got a little drunk and wild at that party and a lot wilder after that. She was hot and heavy for me and still didn't know I was married. That might've cooled her jets, and I didn't want them cooled. With her attention, the grass started looking a whole lot greener on the other side. I wanted to be free, have some time to run around. Shortly after that party, I wanted to be free from my marriage.

Around the holidays, Linda's brother and his family were down from Ohio. She made all these plans: Monkey Jungle with the kids, dinners at our favorite seafood restaurants, playing at the beaches, sailing. All I could think about was Laura, who wanted me to spend Christmas with her. I told Laura that I was working the holiday. That's what I told Linda too, that I needed to work most of the week. Not Christmas day, of course.

She was furious. "Can't you take a couple evenings off? At least have dinner with us? Floyd and Sandy drove all the way down here, and you've spent exactly one evening here so far. One." She held her index finger up.

"I can't just walk away from a case I'm building. I have to be there, show up when I say I will, make a deal here and there, hang out at the bars. You know all this already."

She shook her head. "Every night? I can't believe you have to work on this case every night. Don't drug dealers ever go home? They're at the bar every night? Even they probably have dinner with family around the holidays."

"Think I can get away to go sailing tomorrow morning. How 'bout that?"

She sighed and looked away from me for several seconds. "I'll call the marina and reserve a sailboat. And you better at least be here on Christmas Eve and Christmas."

"I will." Then walls up. Switch flipped. Door closed, right behind me.

Those walls were going to crash down around me. That was inevitable. I was juggling too much: two identities, two women, too many lies. I was having trouble sleeping and eating, my ulcers were on fire, and the scotch wouldn't even settle them. Laura was asking why we always went to her apartment; she wanted to see mine. Finally, I took her to my undercover apartment so she wouldn't get too suspicious. I still hadn't told her I was married with two kids. I was on a train moving so fast, I couldn't stop it, jump off, change directions or even slow it down.

This was how I lived most of my life: letting life take me in a direction with little, if any, forethought or planning on my part. My life unfolded and, no matter what happened, I made the best of things, found the next exciting adventure. Sometimes I was faced with a choice, or a few different options, but I didn't like making tough decisions. In fact, I pretty much avoided them. If I waited long enough, things would just, sort of, fall in place, one way or another. At that time, the train I was on was headed towards a foxy airline stewardess.

Right after New Year's, I came home late, one a.m., drunk as usual. The kids were snoozing away, and Linda was sound asleep in our bed. That night, the silence of the house closed in around me until I actually felt pressure in my chest, like I couldn't catch my breath. Instead of sliding into bed, I opened my dresser drawer, scooped out all my shirts, opened another and grabbed my boxers and socks. Out in the kitchen, I shoved all my clothes in a garbage bag. My heart raced with the thought of Linda waking up, of her coming to see what I was up to. I crept back into our bedroom. Linda hadn't moved. She was such a heavy sleeper; unless one of the kids cried out, then she'd bolt straight out of bed. I slid open the closet and grabbed as many of the clothes as I could in one big armful, hangers and all, and carried them straight to my car, dropping them in the back seat.

When I went back to get the garbage bag, all I could think about was how surprised Laura would be when I showed up at her place with my clothes. I scribbled a note for Linda saying I couldn't take things the way they were and needed some space, some time to get my head straightened out. I folded the paper and tucked it in the mailbox on my way out the door.

When I showed up at Laura's apartment, she was ecstatic.

What I wasn't prepared for was how devastated Linda was. Not sure why that surprised me, we'd been married for twelve years. Don't know what I thought she'd do, jump up and down for joy that I left her. If she'd known where my life was headed, she probably would've. When I came by to see Linda a couple of weeks later, she'd lost so much weight, skinnier than when we'd met twelve years earlier when she was only twenty. It made me sick to my stomach when I saw her wedding ring dangling, literally, on her finger. A man can't feel good about doing that to a woman. Guess I didn't feel bad enough to stay though.

Now I was juggling visits with my family some weekends and seeing Laura when she wasn't flying. Laura wanted me with her on her free weekends, and Linda wanted to know when I was coming back. Between that and work, I was exhausted. After several weeks of this hustle, I finally told Laura that I was married and had two kids but was getting divorced. She was stunned, furious, wouldn't speak to me for days. I finally convinced her that I *did* love her but walking away from a family wasn't that easy. She couldn't believe I'd lied to her for months, and told me that I needed to decide what I wanted.

After several weeks, Laura began asking when my divorce would be final. I hadn't even filed the paperwork yet, but she didn't know that. She also didn't know I'd been thinking about going back home. Partying and getting down with this hot, worldly stewardess had been fun, but when she started talking marriage and babies, well—I already had all that. I didn't need another family. Every time I went back home, I could see how my leaving had upset everyone. I was stuck.

There I was, sitting on the fence—stay with Laura or go back home—when Laura finally realized I hadn't even filed for divorce yet. She flipped out. Again I persuaded her that I needed more time—twelve years I'd been with Linda, had two kids and a home, I told her. She gave me exactly one month and asked me about it every week while she started planning our wedding, picking out invitations, what the ceremony would be like, the works.

By then, I was drinking all day long, which meant I was numb for a good part of my waking hours, and I was a pro at shutting things out. I couldn't strut into a hotel or bar and make a hand-to-hand exchange with a drug smuggler if I was worrying about weddings, divorces, how Rick was doing in school or whether or not Lynn's wrist was broken.

It just didn't work that way; *I* didn't work that way. So, that's exactly what I was doing, ignoring all of it: Laura, wedding plans, Linda, divorce papers, how my kids were doing.

Everything came crashing down on me when Laura wrote a check from my account and forgot to tell me about it, or I didn't write it down. I was terrible with money management, Linda always did all of that: paid bills, balanced the checkbook. Anyways, that check bounced, so the bank called Linda because it was a joint account. She asked the bank who wrote the check, me or her. They told her it was signed by a Laura Burnett.

She called me right away. "Who the *hell* is Laura Burnett?"

The thought was still there that maybe I'd go back home, go back to my old life. If only I could get a different job and get my head straightened out, that was all I needed. And I didn't want our twelve years to end this way; I wanted our marriage to end easily and without any bad feelings or hostility. "What are you talkin' about? I don't know anyone named Laura."

"Is that all you have to say? You don't know anything about her? Is that it? Well, she's writing checks from our account, John."

"The bank probably made a mistake. I'll call 'em and straighten it out."

"Oh please, don't. I already talked to the bank. Enough lies. This explains a lot. Everything, actually. Are you living with her? Is that why you moved out?"

Here we go. She's no dummy. This is how it's gonna end. "Okay. Okay. I didn't think you'd believe me, so I didn't bother tellin' you the truth. But here it is. Laura's this older woman at work who needed some help—"

"Oh, you're right, I *don't* believe you. I'm not buying this load of bullshit! That's what you said years ago when that cadet left her coat in your car, that you were just helping her out, too, giving her a ride home. You've probably been fucking around on me for years. We're getting a damn divorce."

Smack. Dial tone.

Laura had already set the date for our wedding in the fall. Before she found I still hadn't started divorce proceedings, I called an attorney to see how fast he could get me divorced. Life just moved on.

Within a couple of months, Linda and I, or our attorneys, had negotiated divorce and custody terms, and Laura had sent out wedding invitations. When my attorney called to tell me the divorce papers were ready, I went in and signed them. Had several scotches beforehand, so didn't feel a thing.

But I didn't feel much of anything. Never was a feelings kind of guy. Three weeks after my divorce was final, Laura and I were married.

CHAPTER 5
TONY

During the last year I worked undercover, I'd been building a relationship with a man named Tony for several months. We'd made a few small deals, nothing big: several grams of coke here and there. His cocaine was pretty good, so I knew there weren't too many hands between his and a smuggler's. Tony had that air of authority that successful businessmen have, like he could do whatever he wanted, at least whatever money could buy. And he was a businessman: he owned two glitzy tourist shops in West Palm Beach. Dabbling in cocaine came later for him, a little side business—well, a big side business, because anyone working in the cocaine business in South Florida made lots of money. He lived in a fancy townhouse, had a gorgeous girlfriend and drove a black Rolls-Royce.

A couple of the other agents wanted me to get that Rolls-Royce. They thought the Rolls would make a cool undercover car. If Tony delivered drugs in his car, it could be confiscated as evidence, then we could use it later if he was convicted.

I liked Tony. We'd gone to some parties together and had a great time. He even took me to the Playboy Mansion in Chicago for some party he'd been invited to. The Bureau of Narcotics and Dangerous Drugs was trying to build a case against Hefner, so they approved me going to the party. The BNDD, which ultimately became DEA—the Drug Enforcement Agency—couldn't keep up with all the drugs pouring into Miami, so they partnered with local law enforcement, and I was working on that task force. Never saw Hefner or any big drug action at the Playboy Mansion, maybe a line of coke here and there. Did see a lot of liquor and a lot of breasts though. We sure had a lot fun there.

The case against Tony wasn't going anywhere. Lieutenant Williams, who supervised me—big, barrel-chested man who was hard-core on dealers—kept asking me when I was going to close the case and arrest Tony. I stalled for as long as I could. The time, or the situation, was never right to arrest him. It just didn't feel right to arrest him. We arrested smugglers who were shooting at us, killing other smugglers, but Tony wasn't like that. Those violent sons of bitches would then hire some hotshot criminal defense attorney and walk with barely a slap on their wrists. They'd be back out there the next day raking in $300k, half-million dollars a year. All the while, I was putting my ass on the line for about $14,000 a year.

After a long meeting with Williams, in which I did all the listening and he did all of the talking, I was told to arrest Tony and wrap up the case. My one request was to be there during the arrest. When the uniformed officers made the arrest, they'd take me in if necessary, so Tony wouldn't suspect I was a narcotics agent. But I wanted to be there so I could try to control the situation. An arrest situation is tense for everyone, the suspect and the police. I didn't want Tony getting roughed up or making a bad decision and getting shot.

Later that week, I arranged with the department for me to make a hand-to-hand exchange with Tony and gave them the address where it'd go down. I reiterated with the deputies who would make the arrest that Tony didn't carry a weapon, so they wouldn't need to be shooting at anyone.

On the day of the arrest, I wore a wire so the officers would know when to come in and make the arrest. Then I called Tony for some coke but told him my car was in the shop, that I couldn't come get it. I asked if there was any way he could bring it to me. When he agreed, I rattled off the directions to my place, not an undercover apartment but the apartment where Laura and I lived. I don't know what I was thinking. Laura was on a flight to San Francisco so would be gone overnight. At least I'd thought that one through.

When I had him deliver drugs to my own apartment, I'd crossed a line. Before my divorce, there had been another time I crossed the line: took a beat-up informant home to get him cleaned up and try to help him out. In both those incidents, I let the boundary between my life, my real life, and my life posing as a drug dealer get blurry. There's no place in undercover work for blurred judgement. I knew that. When I let Tony deliver drugs to our apartment, when I had taken that informant home, I let those drug dealers into my world. A good narcotics agent never does that.

After Tony slid a packet of coke across the table to me and plucked the money from my hand, I offered him a whiskey. That was the cue to the officers. By the time I set two tumblers on the table, they were pounding on my door. "Police. Open up!"

"What the hell?" Acting the part of a person who was about to get busted, I jumped up and shoved the bag of coke inside the sugar canister.

"Oh fuck, fuck," Tony said, grabbing his briefcase.

"There's a window, back bathroom." I ticked my head in that direction. Wouldn't be my fault if the officers didn't catch him.

More pounding on the door. "Open up. Now!"

To give Tony a head start, I took my sweet time getting to the front door.

He didn't get enough of a head start. The officers nabbed him, and he had a quarter-kilo in his briefcase.

Lieutenant Williams pressured me to provide the prosecutor with information to get a maximum sentence for Tony, but he didn't deserve that, not with smugglers out there who killed for money and drugs. He was truly using coke socially. Sure, he sold a little coke to his friends, but he wasn't a smuggler. The prosecutor wanted to take his car, his townhouse, everything. It just wasn't right. I wouldn't be testifying anyways, to protect my identity, so I provided some basic evidence to the prosecutor and told him that Tony was a small fish, not worth his time.

In the end, Tony got off with only probation. Lieutenant Williams was pissed. He told me to get my act together, even made me take a week off to figure out what the hell I was doing.

I did do a lot of thinking that week, thinking how I wasn't that different from Tony. The only difference was that I was posing as a drug dealer, and Tony really was one. And he was making a boatload more money than I was. Easy money. It wasn't an occasional thought either. My mind stayed on that thought—I am already living the life of a drug dealer.

During that week of mandatory leave, Laura wondered if I should find a different job, said she wanted her husband back—the hilarious, romantic man she'd married. This was the second wife to tell me that I wasn't the man she'd married. Linda was married to me a decade before she told me that, and she knew me better than anyone else in the world, which wasn't saying much. That should've been a sign that my life was getting out of control. But those weren't the signs I paid attention to—signs from unhappy wives. I paid attention to signs from the streets: drug deals, where the big money's flowing to and from, who's bringing in the big loads, who's trusting who.

Laura was also worried about the stress, reminding me that I'd been having nightmares for months. That was true. These were vivid nightmares about my cover getting blown. I woke up those nights in a cold sweat, my heart pounding so bad I thought I was having a heart attack. In these nightmares, the mob discovered my true identity, the mob that was running drugs in and out of southern Florida, the guys who wouldn't think twice about whacking a double-crosser like me. In these nightmares, my time in the Marine Corps was always what gave me away. Somehow the mob would find out who I really was by my service in the Corps.

In my most recurring nightmare, the mob would slice my Marine Corps tattoo off my arm before killing me. Usually my nightmares ended with one of the mob guys pointing at a lampshade and saying, "This is what we do to narcs." Then he threw his head back and laughed maniacally. The lampshade was made of the skin from my arm, sliced so thinly that the light glowed through it, illuminating my tattoo: a black silhouette of the globe, anchor behind it, eagle on top and the words, "Semper Fi." Always faithful.

I didn't know who I was faithful to anymore. To the sheriff's department? Not really. The contrast between the people we were busting, with their millions, and the measly salary we were making to risk our lives, had sapped my enthusiasm for the job. Garbage collectors made the same salary as rookie deputies in Miami in the late 1960s. Was I faithful to the other agents? To Carl for sure. But some agents were getting downright brutal with dealers they arrested, beating the daylights out of them. That was uncalled for.

Sure, we knocked around an informant from time to time. Had to. That's how we kept them scared; they had to be more afraid of not giving us information than they were of getting discovered as a rat. But once someone was arrested and going to jail, there was no need to abuse them. As much as I hated to see that abuse, I couldn't show sympathy to the dealers getting beat up or try to stop the abuse. Those agents would've never tolerated that.

Not only did that whole situation piss me off, it made me question if our department was doing good work anymore.

There were worse things going on. Miami and South Florida police departments, including Dade County, were getting lots of media coverage about corrupt officers. We all knew who the bad ones were, the detectives taking payoffs —drug money in exchange for looking the other way. But no one, including me, was ratting on those dirty officers. Not out of fear of retaliation—though some of those guys were in deep with the drug mobs, scary deep—it was more that police just didn't do that, brothers-in-arms and all that.

The way I saw things, police either stayed clean, squeaky clean, or they were at risk of being bought out. Once a cop took money and didn't get caught, why not take another payoff? One payoff could be equivalent to a detective's yearly salary. For many, it was too lucrative to resist.

I'd been clean up until then. Maybe not squeaky clean, but at least I still had a sense of right and wrong. And I never, not once, took a payoff. Though in hindsight, I think the line between the good guys and the bad guys was getting blurry for me.

Round that time, I talked to the captain about transferring to another department. Good undercover agents took a while to train, and Dade County couldn't keep up with the drug trafficking with the agents it did have. After the captain reviewed my personnel file, he praised all the good work I'd done the past several years, talked about how I was making a real difference out there, how the department needed me, rattled off the awards I'd been given since I joined the force in 1968. In fact, I'd just been given the "Walking Tall" award—that movie had just come out the year before—for detectives who went above and beyond the call of duty fighting organized crime and corruption. He said maybe after I closed all my cases I could request a transfer. Sounded like he'd talked to Lieutenant Williams, since that was always *his* approach: get in, make an arrest, close the case.

The captain wasn't hearing me, wasn't seeing that I wanted out, that I needed out. Nobody was.

CHAPTER 6
THE LAST CHANCE

A few months after arresting—should say, betraying—Tony, I stopped after work at the Last Chance for a drink. Walking over to the bar, I scanned the room to see who was there and was glad the place was mostly empty. Easier to relax. My old supervisor, Bobby, was there at the bar.

Since retiring from the Organized Crime Bureau the year before, Bobby was always on his airboat in the Everglades fishing for largemouth bass and often stopped in at the Last Chance on his way home. Next to him was Karen, one of our longtime informants who knew Bobby when he was on the force. In fact, he processed the paperwork registering her as an informant after I arrested her with several pounds of marijuana. Karen worked at a bar, so she was able to pick up bits and pieces about deals and who was involved. She was a hot young thing and liked the guys. They liked her too, at least the rack she had. The only problem was that she could start blabbing when she drank too much, which she did often. That was a double-edged sword: being talkative made for a useful informant, but also a risky one depending on who she was talking to. She had too much to lose to blow our cover—several pounds would get her some jail time—but I never trusted her very far. Too unpredictable.

"Here's some trouble waitin' to happen," I said, slugging Bobby's shoulder and sliding in next to Karen. Her low-cut tank top was stretched tight across her chest. The sour beer on her breath and her slight swaying as she leaned back to look at me indicated she was tipsy. I ordered a double scotch. My mouth watered as I watched the bartender drop two ice cubes in it.

Few hours later, the bartender shooed us out so he could close up. All three of us were drunk. When I opened the door, the humidity hit me like a wave. Then the salty, musty Everglades smell reminded me where I was, reminded me I hadn't been paying attention to what was going on around me in the bar for the past few hours. That was sloppy. I scanned the parking lot. Empty. Good. I still had a thirty-minute drive back to Cutler Ridge and made a mental note to make sure I didn't get tailed home. I didn't realize back then just how much or how often I let my guard down. Some of those basics—watching my back, staying alert—weren't always automatic anymore.

Bobby motioned for us to follow him to his car. "Come here. Got somethin' to show you guys."

Inside his car, Bobby tugged a bag out that had been duct-taped under his seat. "Want a line of some good shit? This is the best stuff I've ever seen." He looked over at me. "You're still off duty, right?"

I laughed. "A little late to ask that, isn't it?"

"Is it?"

"Come on. You know me better 'an that."

He explained that he'd been trying to put a deal together with this man he knew from Colombia. "Calls himself Miguel. Know him? Ugly-ass guy, dark skin, pock-marks"—he brushed his fingers up and down over his cheeks—"all over his face, crooked teeth? No record yet."

I shook my head and watched Bobby scoop up some coke with his driver's license and dumped it onto a legal pad.

"Good. I was thinking we could put a deal together with him. His stuff is pure, man. We'd make a boatload of money. Karen, roll up a dollar, will ya?" The chunky powder crunched under his license as he chopped and shaped the pile of coke into three thin lines. He swiped the license between his thumb and index finger and sniffed the residue into his nose. After snorting one line, he passed the pad to me.

I snorted a line. "How much are we talkin' about?"

"Kilo. Maybe two. Small enough that we can easily move it through the airport."

I looked over my shoulder. "You in on this too?"

"Sure. You gonna pass that back or what?" She pointed at the coke.

Carefully, I passed the legal pad over the back of the seat to her. The car was silent for a few moments except for the sound of her snuffing up the last line. It was a muggy, hot night and my shirt was clinging to my back. I cranked down the window. The breeze rustled the dry sawgrass surrounding the car and rolled cool across the perspiration on my forehead.

As the cocaine kicked in, my brain began to clear my drunken haze. A white-hot energy, ecstasy, began to expand inside me, breathing life and hope and promise back into me, like when I was in the Marines, like when I was a rookie. "Man, this *is* good shit."

"Yeah," Karen said. "And Miguel's a cool dude. It'll be easy."

Bobby leaned back on the headrest, sniffed hard and cleared his throat. "Just one or two runs. Bring in some good stuff, make a shitload of money. These smugglers make in one day what narcs make in a year, more than that. And we're hardly, well *you're* hardly, makin' a dent in their business here in Miami. Why shouldn't we get in on the action, make some of that easy money? You *know*"—he pounded his fists on the steering wheel—"some of those guys on the force are already smuggling."

"So, what's your plan? Does Miguel know you used to be a narc?"

"*Hell* no. He won't know about you, either. That's what makes this so easy. We fly to Bogotá, but you and me get on and off the plane by ourselves, like we don't even know Miguel. And we'll use our real names, tell customs in Colombia we're down there to fish or buy some of those old Indian motorcycles. Those are real common down there. Hey, we could actually fish for those peacock bass, they're these huge—"

"We aren't fishin' while we're in South America on a drug run."

"Why? We'd be right there. What's the problem? It'd bolster our story."

"You fishin' guys are freaks," Karen chimed in from the back seat.

"This is a drug deal not some vacation, you crazy bastard."

"Okay, okay, you wussy. Anyways, when we go through customs, we shuck and jive about our trip and hide the shit really good in case they search our bags."

"And at U.S. Customs?"

"Same thing. Except there, we show our police IDs. They'll never check the bags of a cop and a retired cop. Why would they? And, if they did, just say we're working undercover."

I stared at him while I calculated the street value of a couple of kilos split four ways. At least $15,000 each. Took me close to a year to make that much money.

"Just think it over. Ain't no hurry. Besides, you're the one with a job to lose."

Maybe because I was drunk or the cocaine had lit me up, or it was the middle of the night out in the boonies, but anything seemed possible. The idea just didn't seem that outlandish. There were other guys on the force involved in smuggling. That, or suddenly they were getting paid a lot more than me, because one bought a huge house and one a brand-new Corvette. Cops can't afford Corvettes.

Me, I'd buy my own sailboat. A big one, not those little twenty-seven-foot schooners that I'd been renting. Maybe buy a house instead of living in an apartment. Not a huge house but a nice one with three bedrooms—so my kids could have their own rooms.

I'd been following rules my whole life—from preacher's son to the Marines to the police force—but the people getting ahead in life were the ones breaking the rules. Why couldn't I bend the rules this once and get ahead a little? Don't get me wrong, I was no goody-two-shoes, but up until that night, I hadn't bent many rules or hadn't bent them very far. I definitely wasn't a dirty cop. Looking back, I believed I could work that little deal and still be one of the good guys.

"I don't gotta think about it. Let's try one run, see how that goes. If nothin' goes wrong, we can try again. Now give me another line of that shit." I cranked my window back up. "And make it a real line this time, not one of those skimpy little things."

As we started making plans, the more genius the idea became. What more perfect way to smuggle drugs into Miami than to do it as a cop? And the only time I'd show my police identification was when we returned to Miami and headed through customs. The rest of the time, that ID would be concealed in my suitcase. For my safety, Miguel and any of his connections in Bogotá would never see that ID. We told Miguel since he had the connection, we'd take the risk of bringing the product through customs. We'd avoid any association or contact with him in and out of the airports, since DEA would be suspicious of any Colombians coming back to Miami a couple of days after flying to Bogotá. That was fine by Miguel; he didn't want to be searched in customs with a stash of cocaine. Then, once we returned successfully with the product, he and Karen would sell it, and we'd all split the profit.

While we worked out the details, whenever a nagging thought popped into my mind about smuggling, I brushed it aside. Told myself, this is such a small load. Two kilos of blow is a drop in the bucket of Miami drug trafficking. The department had evidence rooms, warehouses actually, full of confiscated drugs. Two kilos—half the detectives in Miami were driving around with a few kilos in their trunk on any given day, from arrests just made or evidence headed back to the station or, for some, a payoff from a smuggler. I could almost convince myself this was an undercover op, only this load wasn't going back to the station. But I wouldn't be standing on a street corner selling cocaine, either. Even Miguel and Karen wouldn't be selling it on the streets. We were working at a much higher level. This coke was high-quality stuff that they'd sell to the bigger dealers around Miami. Once word got around about how good our—Karen's and Miguel's—stuff was, we'd be able to move even more on the next run. If I decided to be involved in another run.

Our planning brought to the forefront of my mind how much I really needed out of the undercover work. I kept telling myself that as soon as I completed this one deal with Bobby, then I'd move to another department, maybe put in for a promotion to sergeant. Promotions and a next run never really got reconciled in my mind. They were both rattling around in my head, along with the fact that I could make more money on one drug run to South America than I made in an entire year as a cop.

Things didn't go so well once we got to Colombia. One thing about working undercover is that agents are working in a controlled environment, or at least a known environment, and there's always a fail-safe, a way to step out of the situation if things go bad. And someone, or several people, always have your back. No matter what. Not so on the other side.

It was late when our plane landed in Bogotá, then we spent forty minutes clearing customs and another thirty minutes before Miguel's partner picked us up. By that time, I wanted to wait and get the product in the morning when we could at least see where we were going. But Miguel's partner insisted we not wait until morning, because his contact was expecting us. I hadn't brought my gun, because I couldn't risk getting hung up in customs with a weapon. There we were driving through Bogotá with $10,000 cash and no protection. It felt like a setup to me. All I could rely on was my trust in Bobby. And his trust in Miguel. So, I kept my mouth shut and went along for the ride.

Miguel's connection lived outside of Bogotá and, while the city was similar to Miami in population, it was more sprawled out. We drove thirty minutes or so before the city lights started dwindling, then all that was visible was what our headlights lit up: dirt roads, lots of jungle and run-down shacks tucked into the trees. This was my first time to South America, and I thought it'd be warm and humid like Miami, what with the jungles and all that. I wasn't thinking about how high up in the mountains we'd be. It was cold up there.

We finally arrived at a stucco house, modest by American standards but nice compared to all the shacks we'd driven by. The house was well-lit up on all sides. The driver jumped out, opened a gate then pulled up to the porch. A Doberman pinscher growled low and long at us, its tail and ears straight up on full alert. A man came out, snapped his fingers and the dog instantly sat down and relaxed its ears.

He didn't need the dog anymore; the man had a rifle slung around his shoulder.

As we walked up to the house, the full weight of what I was putting on the line bore down on me: my life, my career, my money. No turning back now, might as well make the best of the situation. As soon as Miguel made introductions, I went into autopilot. I'd done this hundreds of times. Only this time, I wasn't trying to get anything over on anyone. As always, I was concealing that I was an undercover narcotics agent, but that was easy. I'd been doing that every day for years. What was different is that I wasn't trying to convince someone I was a drug smuggler. This time, I was one.

CHAPTER 7
A SNITCH

That deal played out a lot differently than I expected. The South Americans didn't have, or wouldn't sell us, as much cocaine as we'd hoped, only a half-kilo. We couldn't turn it down, we'd come too far. They did a test in front of us, so we knew we were buying pure cocaine, which would be easy for Karen and Miguel to move. We each could still make a few thousand dollars' profit, but we were disappointed to take all that risk for so little return. We had no choice but to buy the half-kilo.

Man, was I relieved to get the hell out of the jungle, past the slums, through the city and back to a motel by the airport.

Bobby and I were surprised at how dense and chunky the coke was. And how good it was. By far, the best cocaine I'd ever snorted. I'd snorted my share of coke undercover, but the stuff on the streets in Miami in the early '70s just wasn't that high-quality. Sometimes it gave me a buzz more like speed: increased pulse, jittery, talkative. Scotch always did the trick for me, so I stuck with that. But this blow must've been pretty pure, having been cooked up recently in a South American jungle.

Over the next couple of hours, Bobby and I chopped it all up so we could scoop it into the cardboard tubes of our clothes hangers. We hated to break up the chunks like that. Karen and Miguel could move the coke faster if dealers saw it in its original state with hardly any powder, clearly uncut. Be we didn't have a choice, that shit wouldn't even go through our paper funnels until we broke it up. Dealers would have to test it to confirm its purity.

When we got tired, we snorted another line. After we filled each tube, we melted candle wax in the ends and stuck the metal hangers back on. Then we hung our shirts over them, not our pants, worried the weight would bend and break the cardboard tubes. We didn't sleep at all that night, ecstatic about the money we were going to make. Karen and Miguel could sell this stuff for good money. All those lines we snorted might've had something to do with my eyes being wide open too.

When Bobby and I deboarded the plane in Miami, we got our luggage and, before we going through customs, I went into the restroom to get my police ID put back in my wallet. While I was in there, I checked to make sure no cocaine was spilling out of the cardboard hangers. I'd hoped it was, so I could get myself a little pinch of coke, a little pinch of courage, before heading through customs, but the wax was holding everything inside the hangers perfectly, just as planned.

I straightened and retucked my shirt, wiped my face and neck with a wet paper towel and smoothed my mustache. This ain't nothin', I told my reflection in the mirror. Even if they found the coke, I'd say it was all part of an undercover operation. Course, if they called Dade County I was screwed, because I wasn't cleared to fly to South America on a case. I'd lose my job, for sure, probably go to prison. Still, better than what I walked into every day on the job—out on the streets. If my cover got blown there, I ended up in a cemetery. Prison was preferable to dead. And close to $4,000 profit was headed my way. More on the next run. Smuggling was a lot like gambling: the chance for a bigger payoff got its hooks in you, and you just kept wanting to try one more time, one more roll of the dice. This time, I'll get the huge payoff, you tell yourself.

The line at customs was short and, lucky day, I got a female customs officer. She was a bit older than me, not bad-looking if a little tough, but women in law enforcement had to be. Looking at her name tag, I said, "How you doin' today, Betty?" I slid my passport, police identification and customs declaration across the counter to her.

She started reviewing my paperwork. "Just fine. What was the purpose of your trip?"

"Went down there looking for some Indian motorcycles. They're cheap as dirt down there and make great racing bikes."

She looked at my ID, then back up at me. "Well, d'you find any?"

"Not any in good enough condition to ship back. It was worth the trip, though cuz I got to meet the prettiest customs officer I've ever seen."

She raised her eyebrows, and I gave her a big old smile. That cracked through her tough shell. We were, after all, on the same team. She slid my ID across the counter, finally smiled back at me and sent me on my way.

When we met up with Karen and Miguel the next day, Bobby and I were ecstatic that we had actually pulled this deal off. We were talking over each other, high-fiving and laughing, just like the old days when he was my supervisor and we'd made a big bust. Karen shook her head and said she still couldn't believe we had the balls to do it. I was floating, partly from our success and partly from the lines we all snorted.

Miguel left shortly after getting his part of the coke, planning to return with our share of the profit in a week. Karen stuck around and had a few drinks with us.

As she was putting the coke into a small duffle bag and getting ready to leave, she said, "Hey, check this out. I got it from a friend, you know, for a little extra protection while I'm selling all this coke." She pulled a Smith & Wesson nine-millimeter from her purse and plunked it on the table between the three of us.

Bobby and I glanced at each other, and I imagined he was thinking the same thing I was: Who the hell did she tell about the cocaine that she needs to carry a gun all the sudden?

I whistled. "That's a big gun for a little thing like you. Can you even rack that slide?"

"You mean, like, cock it?"

I nodded.

"It's a little hard, but I can do it." She took a few gulps from her beer and struggled to pull the slide back, the gun pointing this way and that. She's gonna kill one of us with that damn thing, I thought.

"Lemme have a look at that." I turned the barrel towards the wall and slid the gun from her hands. I ejected the magazine and pulled the slide back. The chamber was empty and pretty clean. Either someone had taken good care of that Smith & Wesson or it hadn't been shot in a while. That gun was way too big for her; more of a menace than protection. She was more likely to shoot herself.

I leaned down and slid my PPK out of my ankle holster. "Here's what you need to get. A small pistol that fits in your hands." I handed the gun to her. "And keep that thing pointed away from us, alright?"

As soon as she wrapped her hand around the grip, she looked up and smiled. "Oh, that *does* feel better. This'd fit in my purse better too." She leaned forward, fully aware that her cleavage was showing. "Hey, I'll swap mine for yours."

"For your what?" I grinned.

Bobby chuckled. "Save it for after I leave."

"My gun. Unless there's somethin' else you wanna swap?" She bit on her lower lip, giving me her sexy look.

I took my eyes off her breasts and back to her face. "I'll trade you my PPK for that Smith & Wesson if you want, but that's it. I'm a married man." I lifted my glass, offering a toast to the deal.

"Aww. You're no fun." She tapped her bottle of beer to my glass, then took a long swig. "I'll take your pistol though. What's it called again?"

"A PPK. And I'd like it back. Bring it when you come back with our money."

"Which will be when?" Bobby asked.

"Uh, let's see. How about we check back in … three

weeks? Should give me plenty of time to move all this stuff." She pointed at the duffle bag.

"Can we make it two? Two weeks?" Bobby asked.

Good idea, I thought. Three weeks was a long time to be waiting on our money.

She agreed, then headed out with her quarter-kilo and my PPK. Bobby and I each kept a little stash for ourselves, just a hundred grams.

That week, I started scouting around for a sailboat to put a down payment on, telling Laura I was expecting a bonus from the department for a longstanding case I was finally closing.

When Karen showed up two weeks later, she looked like shit: tired, pale, nervous, talking a mile a minute. We knew right away she'd been snorting a lot of that coke. She handed each of us envelopes, apologizing there was only $500 in them, promising she'd get us the rest of our money, at least $3,000 each, in another week or two. She paced around the room, giving us some bullshit story about an ex-boyfriend stealing the coke and how she was worried he might try to hurt her or kill her but wouldn't explain why. Her story didn't make any sense. What I figured was she got greedy, sold enough to her "ex-boyfriend" to get plenty of money for herself, snorted a bunch, then cut the rest so much that she had a hard time selling any more of it.

Bobby and I were so fucking pissed. If she had any of the coke left, which I doubted, it was probably crap now. And if it hadn't been cut to shit, we couldn't go out and sell it ourselves. She had us over a barrel, and she knew it: we weren't going to see any more money, and if we gave her a hard time, pushed her too hard, she'd threaten to rat us out.

We'd never get our money out of her. There went my damn sailboat.

I was so mad about not getting my money, I never even thought about my PPK. That, it turns out, was my biggest mistake.

CHAPTER 8
EASY MONEY

The only thing that crossed my mind much at the time was that easy money. I'd crossed that line—smuggled as a cop—but didn't get my big payoff. Bobby and I were already scheming about another larger run, only now we didn't have enough money to buy another load. Miguel thought his connection might give us some cocaine on the arm—front it to us and we'd pay them later—but we had to have someone else reliable to distribute it for us in the States. Miguel didn't think he could move more than a kilo and we definitely weren't messing around with Karen again. We needed someone who could hold up their end of the deal, someone who could move a kilo of cocaine fast and without snorting a bunch of it. Unfortunately, all the potential dealers we knew were from our undercover work. I couldn't mix my undercover connections with my smuggling operations. This all had to be done completely separate from anything I was working on for Dade County. After all, I was still a cop.

What made our plan so foolproof, a cop walking

through U.S. Customs with a couple kilos of cocaine on him, was also what made it so complicated. We were double-playing this: hiding from Miguel and the Colombians that we were police, then using our identities as detectives to walk the stuff through customs, then finding someone who didn't know we were police to distribute it. And of course, all without the department knowing what I was doing. There were too many variables that could go wrong. The biggest risk was blowing my undercover identity, in which case the Colombians would most likely kill me, or our distributor here stateside would rat me out.

Before we reached any decisions about our next move, I was called into a meeting with Lieutenant Williams. Sitting in there with him was an Internal Affairs officer. I hated those tight-asses with their suits and ties, policing the police. What the hell did they know about our work and how we were putting our life on the line every day? Wish they'd just let us do our damn jobs. The Internal Affairs guy was in my face about a PPK that a woman, who was involved in a homicide case, had in her possession. A PPK registered in my name.

I put my hands up in front of me and pumped them, trying to put the brakes on where this conversation was headed. "Whoa, whoa. Slow down here. If you're talkin' about Karen Wilder, she's one of our informants. Look it up. I registered her as an informant maybe ... eighteen months, two years ago. I *did* give her my PPK. About a month ago. She was lookin' for a gun smaller than this big ol' Smith & Wesson nine-millimeter. It was a simple favor I did for her. She was worried someone was after her. She's a good informant and, you know"—I looked, pointedly, over at

Williams—"that we do whatever it takes to nurture a good informant. Just business as usual. But I will say, I haven't seen her for a couple of weeks so … I don't know what she's been up to." I tossed my hands out and shrugged.

Mr. Internal Affairs was scribbling furiously on a notepad.

"Well, was she arrested for homicide?" I asked.

"Nope. Claims she witnessed one though. Committed by an ex-boyfriend."

Here we go, I thought. Who knows what she's gotten into now. Maybe her ex-boyfriend *had* been trying to kill her.

"Miami Beach police questioned her about a concealed weapon she had on her person. She said she was carrying it because this guy, her ex, was after her. Miami Beach ran the serial number." Internal Affairs stared at me, eyebrows raised. "Turns out the gun's registered in your name." He points at me.

I wanted to reach out and break his skinny little finger. "Yeah, you said that already. Don't know nothin' about this. She's a small-time dealer, probably does a little hookin' on the side. She'll do anything for a little money. Probably got herself into trouble with the mob or some drug dealers. All I did was lend her my gun. She was scared, didn't seem like a big deal to give her a gun that at least fit her hand."

The next week, what's-his-face from Internal Affairs was back. They had brought Karen in for more questioning. Sounds like she got scared and started blabbing about a bunch of murders she'd supposedly witnessed—don't know who the hell this ex-boyfriend was, obviously a real nice guy—and how she had a price on her head because of what she knew. Then she told them all about my trip to Bogotá. Everything. Told them I was pressuring her to sell the cocaine. The little snitch. No wonder someone had a hit on her.

The department had found evidence that a drug mob did, in fact, have a hit on Karen's head, so she was now under heavy police protection as a witness in the homicide case. My instincts told me she was running scared with this homicide, probably aided and abetted her boyfriend in the murder. She was spilling her guts about anything, frantic to keep herself out of trouble and, apparently, alive. I was just another bit of information she was throwing at the detectives to deflect attention away from her or, at least, to muddy the waters.

Internal Affairs was all over my ass. "She's offering sworn testimony that you were in Bogotá a few months ago and came back with a half-kilo of cocaine."

"Ah, that bitch is just pissed cuz she's in some kinda trouble. She'll say anything to stay outta jail."

"Yeah? Well, why don't you tell me about your trip to Colombia."

I stared at him. *Fuck! Hope someone does get that little snitch.*

"The one Karen told us about. Have you been to Colombia recently?"

Just play this real cool, I told myself. "Yeah, I went down there a few months ago. Despite what Karen told you, it didn't have nothin' to do with drugs. Just a vacation."

"Hmm. Took the wife and kids to Bogotá, huh? Sounds like a great family vacation."

All it'd take for them to discover I went there was to pull the airline records. "Nah. Bobby and I went fishin' for some of those peacock bass down there. Looked around for old Indian racing motorcycles. They got a lot down there. And cheap. Love those things. Man, they're fast. You can make a pretty penny too if—"

"You got any proof of that, John? Couple of Indians in your garage?"

I shook my head. "Couldn't find any worth the cost to ship 'em back."

"John"—he stared at me for a beat—"she's offering sworn testimony."

"What the hell do you want me to say here? It's her word against mine. Isn't the department gonna back me up? I've worked here for seven years, puttin' my ass on the line every day for Dade County. Doesn't that count for anything?" I looked at Williams, who hadn't said a thing and now wouldn't make eye contact with me. That's how I knew the department was screwing me on this.

"We'll need to start an internal investigation. Next week."

Racking my brain, I couldn't think of any other trails I left that could implicate me. They wouldn't have any proof of what Bobby and I'd done in Colombia, just two airline tickets that proved we went there. All they had was Karen's testimony. And my damn PPK. My gun didn't prove anything; it was just another link between me and Karen. Should've never given her my gun. An investigation could result in criminal charges against me, but I doubted it. All that Internal Affairs had was hearsay on Karen's part, her word against mine. And Bobby's. He'd vouch for me.

I had a nagging thought in the back of my mind that maybe she'd been wearing a wire when she last met with me and Bobby. She'd been acting really suspicious, nervous, jittery. I'd assumed it was all the coke she'd probably been snorting and the fact that she didn't have our money. My instincts were never that far off, but I *had* been a little careless lately. Karen was a wild card.

At the time, there was a lot of political pressure on Dade County about the growing problem with dirty cops. I wasn't the worst dirty cop on the force, but with a witness, an investigation would likely lead to me being fired, possibly prosecuted. They'd have to make a big show out of this, how they're rooting out the corruption. And I'd be the one on stage, hanging high and dry with no support from Dade County. My name and face would be all over the papers. If I stayed.

If I left, they'd probably make some half-assed investigation then just bury it all.

I was furious. But I wasn't stupid. Internal Affairs had no choice. So I had no choice.

Two days later, I resigned from the Department. Just like that, seven years of my life, seven years of service to Dade County—award-winning service—was gone.

As soon as I resigned from the force, I wanted out of Miami. Away from the crime and the drugs and the violence. Away from the person I was becoming. That city, and that undercover life, had consumed me: it was a big part of my first marriage falling apart and was definitely the reason I worked that deal with Bobby and Karen. If I hadn't been an undercover agent, I wouldn't have had the first clue how to smuggle drugs. But by then, I was a pro at smuggling, and that easy money and excitement were calling to me. There was no way I could stay in Miami and keep my nose clean. I knew it. Knew it in my gut. That city was bad news when I was a cop, and it was going to be bad news now that I wasn't one.

We moved up to North Carolina and stayed with my folks for a week until we found an apartment. What a miserable, long week that was. My folks didn't believe in divorce, and here I was with my second wife, who was pregnant. Whenever I was alone with my mother, she'd mumble this or that about me getting back to church, praying, divorce. I could see the judgement all over her frowning face.

I got a job driving trucks for a dynamite-blasting crew, making about the same money I'd made as an agent. But with Laura not working—airlines didn't allow pregnant women to work back then—I barely made ends meet. Hadn't sent Linda child support for months. That's no way to live: not able to support a family, not to mention two of them.

Started getting these crippling headaches that the doctor called cluster headaches. He gave me some pain pills but said the best way to stop them was to reduce my stress. What a joke. I'd just left one of the most stressful jobs I could imagine, made doubly stressful by the smuggling I tried to do as a cop. Now I am just driving a truck and can't handle the stress? The stress, I realized, was about the money. Or the lack thereof.

A year later, when our daughter, Julie, was about six months old, Laura suggested we move back to Miami. Her old airline hub was down there so she could easily get work and her parents could watch Julie. The idea of being back in a big city with more job opportunities gave me some hope, and I figured I'd gotten that whole smuggling fantasy out of my system.

Being back by the ocean and closer to Rick and Lynn again was nice. Right away, I found a job as a car salesman. Figured I'd like the interaction with people, the socializing and convincing a person to believe, well, whatever I wanted them to believe about a car out there on the lot. That, I could do very well.

My new co-worker, Alfredo, was a scrawny, fast-talking dude with wild curly hair. His Spanish sounded more Colombian than Cuban. As we left the car lot one evening, he invited me out for a drink. While we waited for our drinks, Alfredo was fidgeting and glancing at me from the corner of his eye. It was unnerving, because I knew what it felt like to be checked out. I searched my memory to recall whether I'd ever busted anyone in that area of Miami. Alfredo wasn't a familiar face, and I always remembered the faces, not the names—crooks were always changing those—but always remembered the faces.

"What's goin' on here, Alfredo?"

He took a long swig of his beer, swallowing loudly, then turned towards me. "Okay. Okay. I wonder if … if you … want to make some more money? The car lot, is not always the best money, no? I have a good plan for us."

"What'd you have in mind?"

He glanced around us and leaned in. "I have, how you say, conexiones, mi familia, in Colombia. If you can sell some weed, maybe sometimes some coca, we can make good money."

I held his gaze for a minute to make sure I wasn't being setup, that I wasn't being sloppy this time. Then I stared down at my scotch, swirled that amber liquid around in the glass, took a sip. Tony came to mind, that man I'd arrested just before quitting the force. I thought about Tony's leisurely lifestyle, his money, the integrity and loyalty I saw in him and how he balanced running a business with a little cocaine dealing on the side. I fantasized about having as much money as he had, investing in a company or two that could make money for me then, if I wanted to, keep an intermittent cocaine business on the side. I saw myself with all the free time I wanted, my own sailboat (finally) and a big house, not a mansion, but nice-sized with a pool and a big slide for all three of my kids.

If I made one good deal, maybe two, I'd be set. I knew exactly how to keep from getting caught. I'd know when we were being watched or sense when something wasn't right. What I knew about undercover narcotics surveillance would come in real handy in a smuggling operation. And now that I was no longer an agent, smuggling would be less dangerous for me.

I took another sip of scotch, looked back up at him, pursed my lips and started nodding. "Let's keep talkin'. Work out some details. See what we can put together."

CHAPTER 9
TWO MILLION QUAALUDES

A few weeks after that conversation, I was at Alfredo's house with five other people plotting how to smuggle twenty, thirty bales of marijuana into Miami from Colombia, who would pay for what and who would do what. Too many people were involved, all of us strangers with no trust, everyone conniving for a bigger share of the pie, which would've been maybe $450,000. Good smuggling requires good business, but that was some bad business going down in that room. My gut was telling me to pull out, that the $90,000 I stood to earn wasn't worth the risk. In the end, we couldn't reach any agreement, so the deal fell through.

My mind kept churning on how to make a deal with Alfredo work, about the other side, the side I used to be on, and the people who were still fighting the drug traffic—Carl had left the department shortly after me, which was a relief. Thought about every move agents would be making and every move I needed to make to avoid getting caught. I could easily spot a surveillance. I knew how to smuggle drugs and knew that anyone in the drug business could make lots of money if it was done right. That's exactly what I intended to do: make a lot of cash, quick and easy, invest all of my money and get out after a few runs.

On the next opportunity with Alfredo, I insisted we involve people who trusted each other. The problem was, anyone I knew who could move any product would to be someone I knew from my old life as a narcotics agent. But I needed someone who'd believe I was legitimately trying to put together a deal, that this wasn't a setup. And someone who didn't have a grudge against me from my time as a narc, someone I'd never arrested or used as an informant.

Charlie was an informant used by other agents briefly, but he quickly disappeared from the streets. Assumption in the department was that Charlie had left the "business" to avoid being used by detectives as a snitch. Now those were the kind of principles I felt comfortable working with: someone who could not easily be coerced into ratting. He was a real laid-back kid, maybe mid-twenties, loved to surf, so always had a dark tan, sun-bleached hair. He didn't care for high-stress situations, dealers who lied, cheated and stole. With Charlie, what you saw was what you got. Getting into the smuggling world as an ex-narc was so risky for me, I needed to work with people who were easy for me to read. Charlie fit that bill. And a few years earlier, he moved a lot of product, mainly to the young, rich crowd in West Palm Beach: college students and beach bums still living off their wealthy parents.

Charlie and I sat down to talk business. He wasn't inter-ested in getting back into small-time dealing, he was only willing to go back into the business if the payoff was big.

He was hoping for a big break, the kind of break Alfredo and I were offering. And I needed his assurance that no one but him would ever know I used to be an agent.

"I got no problem with that," Charlie said. "The past is the past. Let's move on and see what we can put together."

"Let's do it. All we need's a moneyman and a pilot," I said.

"Oh, is that all?" he said, and we both laughed.

"Actually, that's *exactly* what we need."

"Think I know just the guy for the money. He's kinda new to the scene. Larry. Moved down from New Jersey a few years ago." This was good news, ruled out any chance that I had any prior contact with this Larry guy when I was undercover. "He's got a huge op already, wheelin' and dealin' from Miami to West Palm. I move some stuff for him every couple months. He's got some fancy car and even a driver, so I bet he's got a pilot or can get one. How 'bout I meet with him, see if he's interested. If he is, we'll all sit down and see how it feels."

That's what I wanted to hear. He understood the importance of instinct and gut feeling and finding the right people. Smugglers and dealers were all over Miami, but I wasn't going to work with just anyone.

Within a week, me, Alfredo and Charlie sat down with Larry and his pilot, Ron, to talk about working together. Larry showed up in a red Maserati—his driver waited in the bar while we all had lunch. Larry looked Italian with slicked-back almost-black hair, dark eyes, and one of these strong, curved Roman noses. He was dressed to the nines in a business suit. No doubt in my mind, he was connected to the mob up in Jersey. Ron was serious, calculating, all focused on landing strips and navigating in bad weather and shit like that. Precisely what you want in a pilot.

Charlie could move at least 3,000 pounds of pot every couple of months, an amount Alfredo knew his family connections could produce. Ron knew of a Douglas DC-3 for sale, which could easily transport that much marijuana and more, though it'd need to be retrofitted with additional fuel tanks. Even with extra fuel, we'd still have to refuel somewhere in the islands between South America and Florida.

I raised the question about carrying weapons. As an undercover agent, I'd seen smugglers get killed trying to shoot their way out of an arrest. If my new partners were ready to kill for this, I'd have second thoughts about working with them. I'd carry a gun because, even with all the turnover in the Miami smuggling scene, it was possible I'd run into someone who knew (besides Charlie) that I'd been a policeman: maybe an old informant or someone I'd arrested. Of course, I wasn't explaining this to my partners.

"I want to be on the up and up with you guys," I said. "I do plan to carry a pistol, just in case some other smugglers try to rip us off or a deal goes south. There's lots of cash and merchandise at stake here. But, if we ever get caught, which I don't expect to happen, I don't want any part of a shoot-out with DEA. Not sure if any of you'll be packin' too, but I'd like to get that out on the table now. "

Alfredo made a surrender motion, hands in the air. "No gun for me. Don't know how to use one. Don't want to."

"Me neither," Charlie said, shaking his head. "But I'll tell you, if we ever get caught, I'll bolt if I can. I can be a quick little bastard."

"I always have a gun when I fly," Ron said. "Keep it in the plane. Hope it never comes to this, but I'm not interested in a showdown with any pigs either. I'm with John on that. We ever get caught, we get caught. No shooting our way out of a bust."

That put my mind at ease, that we had a code we would follow: no one ever got violent.

Ron looked over at me then. "Let's go target-shooting sometime. Bet I'm a better shot than you."

"Wanna put some money on that?" I said, grinning. Charlie was looking at me, probably wondering why the hell I'd want to show off my experience with guns.

Larry spoke up then. "Well, I always carry because I always have cash. But I'll be an arm's reach from all the ops. I'll buy the plane, but I'm sure as hell not unloading it." He let out a deep belly laugh, though he was not kidding, not even in the slightest.

Larry was the moneyman. Even more than Charlie had described to me a week earlier, Larry was filthy rich. That Maserati was just one of his cars, his favorite one. He lived in a mansion in West Palm Beach and had plenty of cover businesses he could use to launder our drug money. The start-up of our operation was all financed by him: he bought the DC-3, the cargo trucks, paid for all of our hotels on every run and the majority of the cost of the drugs we purchased in Colombia. We all had to pitch in some money, and the more you put in, the more profit you made. But Larry was the moneyman, so he was in charge; he gave us part of his profit for the risk we took flying the drugs into Florida and distributing them. He called the shots. Larry had the final say on how much we flew in, where we sold it, everything. And he never came too close to the drugs, so his risk was mainly a financial one.

Ron and I studied flight-plan maps of the Florida coast southeast of Orlando where I knew small planes, if they flew low enough, could dip under the FAA's radar and where there were farmers who'd let planes fly into their empty fields for the right price. All information I knew from my days as an agent. Ron analyzed maps of northern Colombia, calculating the nautical miles between the small airports around Orlando and the jungles outside Cartagena, where we'd fly into. With extra fuel tanks inside the plane, we could fly there without refueling, but once we had the plane loaded with marijuana—bales were fifty pounds each —we'd have to refuel on the way home. Next came maps of the Bahama Islands, where Ron had a contact we could make arrangements with to pay for barrels of fuel next to a landing field.

After months of preparation, everything was a go. Alfredo and Ron would fly to Colombia to meet his family's connection.

Before making any cocaine or marijuana exchanges, the Colombians asked us, as a favor, to move some Quaaludes they had manufactured—two million of them. We hoped the Colombians would sell us marijuana, but we needed to nurture this connection. I knew how to do that. We had to move slowly, patiently building their trust. This connection might have been tight with Alfredo's family, but they didn't know us Miami gringos from any of the other dozens of smugglers trying to move product on boats or planes from South America up to Florida.

I took months and months to get rid of all those pills,

selling them to every dealer we knew. Charlie had built a false room between his house and garage. We crammed ourselves in there and counted Quaaludes—one at a time, one hundred per baggie—out of a barrel, our hands covered with Quaalude powder, breathing and coughing the bitter dust.

We had everyone in Miami selling them. Now, we weren't selling them by the capsule to high-school kids or shit like that; we were selling them to dealers, wholesale, five thousand at a time, I think for a buck a pill. It was such a pain in the ass. I was so fed up with Quaaludes. They were a popular sedative, known for making girls horny, but they just weren't as easy to get rid of as pot. But this was a favor to the Colombians, and a test, I'm sure, to prove that we were legit. And I did make close to $50,000 after Larry took his percentage. Not a bad return for a few months' work. Enough of a profit to give me my first taste of that easy money I'd been craving. And after that first run, nothing went bad, so we all knew we could trust each other. That's all that mattered, gut instinct. And that easy money.

Every few months, we brought in a load of drugs from Colombia, mostly pot, sometimes a few kilos of cocaine. After a couple of successful runs, I quit my job at the car dealer. Told Laura I started buying and selling gemstones, even brought a couple of emeralds back from Colombia each trip. Those were fun to buy—big, uncut emeralds that I'd haggle a good price for.

I'm pretty sure Laura suspected I was up to something, but I was a pro at living double lives and she was gone for days at a time, more if she was flying an international trip. And I'm sure she liked the money. We'd been living on, at

best, $20,000 a year for the past few years, always strug-
gling to make ends meet. We bought a house, paid off my
truck and bought her a new car. Even gave Linda a nice
wad of cash now and then; I'd been behind on child
support for years.

On each drug run, Ron and Alfredo flew to Colombia,
while Charlie and I stayed in a motel in Florida, near our
landing strip. Our job was to prepare the makeshift runway
where the plane would land that night. We couldn't land in
broad daylight, and we certainly weren't landing at any
airports.

In the DC-3, it took around eight hours to get to
Colombia and eleven or twelve coming back loaded down
with marijuana. With extra fuel tanks, we only had to refuel
once on the way back to Florida—flying with that kind of
payload really sucked up the fuel. We had to check the
weather forecast between Florida and Colombia before any
take offs or landings. No air-traffic control for smugglers.
We didn't even try to bring a load in during hurricane
weather.

On one particular run, we waited for close to a week
before the weather cleared enough to fly out of Florida. By
the third day, we were pacing the rooms of the hotel. We
had three rooms, two adjoining, and dragged tables into
one room so we could play poker, drink and watch Miami
Dolphins games. The curtains were always drawn and the
windows shut, the air conditioner on full blast. We lowered
our voices and whispered about the shipment and the
plane, hangared at a nearby private airport. We hung out in
the lobby and lounge too, just to get out of the rooms.

By day four, I was nervous about being in the same

hotel—five men coming and going—for so long. The room could've been bugged, though I checked for a mic whenever we'd been gone. When Alfredo picked up the phone to call his family in Colombia, I said, "You probably shouldn't use the phone in here."

"Por qué?"

"Taps. Cops might've tapped the phone line."

He dropped the phone back into its cradle. "How?" Everyone looked at me.

I shrugged. "I don't know. They do it all the time in the movies. That's how pigs get info on smuggling ops, right? Like when we went out for dinner last night. Just shouldn't take any chances."

Charlie spoke up. "Alfredo, let's call from the pay phone in the lobby, see what the weather's like over there."

For the next twenty-four hours, we went through rolls of quarters calling South America from the lobby pay phone. When the weather was clear in Cartagena, a storm raged in Miami. When the storm cleared, Cartagena was socked in. Larry was getting ready to call the trip off and send us all back home.

Near the end of the week, I returned from the lobby with Ron for the third time that day, knocked once, paused, then rapped three more times. Larry unlocked the door. I closed and locked the door behind me and peered out between the curtains. I was sure the front-desk clerk was getting suspicious.

"Weather's good now for two days in Colombia," Ron said. "Clear here through the weekend too. Let's get to the airport."

By then, it was Friday. I was supposed to pick up Lynn

and Rick for a weekend visit. I glanced at the phone, but I didn't have time for an argument with Linda. Charlie and I needed to go check into another hotel closer to the field where Ron would land, rent a cargo truck, get the pickup with all the gear and be ready the next evening to set up a makeshift landing strip. I'd have to come up with a good explanation later for missing my weekend visit. I reached past the phone, drained a glass of scotch and hustled out the door after Charlie.

Late the next evening, we drove the thirty-five miles to the location where the plane was to land. We drove onto a gravel road that paralleled a long field. Some remnant stubble from sugarcane harvested years ago jutted up from the dirt. On the other side of the field was thick sawgrass with a few cypress trees and, beyond that, a marsh.

Charlie pulled the cargo truck off the road alongside one end of the field, and I pulled the pickup truck off the road about a quarter-mile past the cargo truck. We each began unloading wooden crates containing black steel pots, each one about the size of a gallon jug of milk. Wide wicks stuck out the top of each pot, which we would light to make a temporary runway for the plane. The oil sloshed around as I lugged the crates into the field.

We began pushing the steel pots into the dirt, constantly checking the road for headlights, listening for any cars driving down the road. Charlie was setting up his smudge pots at the other end of the field, us both working towards each other. Once we met up in the middle of that row, we paced off two hundred feet and began setting up a parallel row on the other side of the field. We did this as fast and quiet as we could, occasionally stumbling over an old sugarcane clump.

After about thirty minutes, me and Charlie finished a U-shaped formation with a hundred smudge pots: two parallel rows, 2,500 feet long, ran north and south, twenty-five pots in each row, then several smudge pots connected the south end of the two rows, forming the U shape.

Sweat was streaming down my temples and, after jogging back over to the truck, I was panting. We moved both trucks behind a dilapidated shed and grabbed the hand-to-air radio from the pickup. Then we trudged back to the area with dense sawgrass and cypress trees to wait.

Within seconds the mosquitoes descended on us. I looked at my watch. "Should hear from them soon," I said, slapping a mosquito on my neck.

"Fuckin' mosquitos," Charlie said, swatting back and forth in front of his face. The mud made a sucking sound as he shifted his feet around. He situated himself on the bulky roots that protruded from the base of a cypress tree.

I swiped my hand into a fist in front of my face. "These skeeters are gonna eat us alive."

For the next half hour we squatted on the bulging cypress roots until our legs felt like they were being poked with pins and needles, then we stood and leaned back on the tree trunks, trying to keep out of the mud. The mosqui-toes whined constantly in my ears. Just when I thought I couldn't take the heat and humidity and mud and mosquitos any longer, couldn't wait another minute, when pant legs and shoes were soaked, the radio finally crackled.

That was the best sound I'd heard in a long time.

Instantly, the frogs stopped croaking. Ron's voice squawked from the radio. "At the coastline. Five minutes away. Over."

"All's clear. Over," Charlie said.

We each ran to a row of pots and began lighting the wicks from the south to the north as the plane's engines droned louder and louder. Then, we stumbled back to the edge of the field until the plane was right overhead, then raced into the field behind the plane, extinguishing the smudge pots, south to north again, as the plane landed. The less time the smudge pots were lit, the better.

We jogged up to the plane's cargo door as Alfredo dropped it open and climbed down the steps.

"How'd it go? What'd you get?" I asked.

Alfredo shoved into each of our arms a few long, narrow boxes wrapped with tape. "Is called mother of ... how you say in English, 'perla?' Is mother of ..."

"Mother-of-pearl," Ron said from up in the cargo door, handing more boxes down to us. "Wait 'til you see it. Man, it's beautiful stuff. Uncut. Twenty kilos." He grabbed the last of the boxes too, and we all hustled to the truck.

Once the boxes were loaded into the truck, Ron said, "I'll get the plane back to the hangar. See you guys at the hotel."

He and Alfredo ran back to the plane as Charlie and I lit the smudge pots again. After the plane took off between the rows of flames, we ran behind it, once more, extinguishing the pots, sticking them into the wooden crates and loading it all into the back of the pickup.

When we were all back at the rendezvous location, including Larry, Alfredo slit the tape and opened up a box of the cocaine. There was hardly any powder; it was mainly chunks of cocaine with a faint, iridescent pink color. Alfredo was beaming as he plucked a couple of the smaller pieces out and chopped them into powder with his driver's license. After snorting a line with a rolled-up dollar bill, he passed the tray to Larry. The tray made it all around the room and so did the smiles.

As the euphoria spread through my body, I fully understood the value of uncut cocaine. This was better, by far, than what Bobby and I'd purchased in Bogotá. One line had me feeling seven feet tall, like I could do anything in this life I wanted to. Anything. The world was mine.

"Man, this is some good stuff. Best I ever snorted. No shit," Charlie said.

A big, loose grin spread across Alfredo's face. "Mi familia gets the *best* coca."

"We're gonna get rich off this stuff," I added.

High-quality cocaine like that was hard to come by, at least at the scale we were looking to purchase, in the late '70's. Marijuana was much easier to get in large quantities. That whole South American cocaine production and export system wasn't that organized yet. But this cocaine had come from the very top, right out of the jungle. When I'd busted someone with drugs that had a high percentage of the original substance—heroin, cocaine, whatever—I knew I was moving up the food chain as far as smugglers were concerned. Because, as drugs moved out into the distribution network, everyone cut it, so they could make more money. With every cut, the quality decreased.

But this stuff was pure cocaine. When we delivered this to our distributors, they'd move it lightning-fast and come running back for more. If we could keep buying cocaine instead of marijuana from Alfredo's family, we'd be rolling in dough.

Between the cocaine I'd just snorted and the promise of things to come, I'd arrived. Finally. I was on top of the world and wasn't a thing that could keep me from my spot there. Nothing.

CHAPTER 10
CONVAIR 440

Smuggling wasn't scary. Nerve-wracking maybe, but not scary. When you're smuggling, you have to be vigilant. You can't get sloppy or put your guard down. In law enforcement, it was the same exact thing. It was kind of a catch-me-if-you-can game. I loved every second of that game. It was so exciting to see if you could get the drugs into the country without getting caught, while DEA is trying to catch you.

Coming up with different ways to get it into the country was really a challenge for me. I guess because you aren't supposed to do that, but if you're really good at it, you can. It'd be a fun game even if you didn't make any money at it. Though I was making a lot of money.

Seeing if you can catch drug smugglers was just as challenging. Someone ought to come up with a game about smuggling, a board game or something that could capture the intensity, the excitement, the strategizing, the potential for huge payoffs. They'd make a fortune.

And the cocaine, the uncut Colombian, God, it was good stuff. I was loving that too.

The motel we stayed in this time while waiting for the delivery was about thirty-five miles from the field where they'd land the plane. Leading up to the motel was a long driveway, maybe three, four hundred yards long. At the far end of the driveway on one side, mostly concealed by a fence, was an auto-salvage yard. The room looked out over the driveway, which is what we wanted, so we could see if any cop cars pulled into the parking lot.

Ron and Alfredo were stuck in Colombia waiting for the marijuana delivery. Once they finally had the plane loaded, it'd be another ten hours before they arrived. Charlie and I killed time in the hotel playing cards, watching TV and listening to the radio.

Around six p.m. Charlie rattled a bottle of black pills at me. "Hey, you want some of these?"

I recognized the black beauties—speed—in the bottle. Lots of dealers were selling those things like candy when I was a cop. Never liked them. The buzz I got from amphetamines was somewhere between the effect of drinking way too much coffee and snorting bad, heavily-cut cocaine.

"They'll make the night go by faster. And if they take"— I shook my head and tapped my finger to my pursed lips— "ah, if we finally get called in to work … you know … in the middle of the night, we'll be good to go."

What the hell. What else are we gonna do all night? I motioned for him to give me one. He dropped two in my palm, and I swallowed them with a sip of scotch.

Much later that night, long after the speed had kicked in, a fat orange moon rose on the horizon behind the hotel. Charlie kept peeking out the window, nervous to begin with and now hyperalert from the speed. He was making *me* nervous. My heart was already racing and my palms and armpits sweating from the speed. Hell, those black beauties were even making my scalp itch. "Stay away from that damn window, will you? C'mon, let's play another round of poker. Double or nothin'."

Still looking through a slit in the curtains, Charlie leaned his face closer and strained to see in the distance. "Shit. I think the pigs are out there watchin' us. There's a buncha cop cars out there." He grabbed his wallet and keys off the table.

I pulled the curtain back. Sure enough, three or four cars were parked out near the end of the driveway.

We bolted to the bathroom and squeezed out the bathroom window, scattering into the surrounding woods. Squatting in the bushes where I could see the hotel, I listened and watched for anyone, anything. No movement around the hotel, no one following us into the woods, not even the sound of footsteps or a car door opening or a police radio crackling. Not a thing.

We hunkered down in our hiding spots for half an hour, then Charlie inched over next to me and whispered, "Think we can get to our cars and get the hell outta here?"

All that adrenaline was wearing off and so were the amphetamines, thank God. If those *were* cops, they'd have searched our hotel room by then. There wasn't any evidence in there to arrest us anyways. We hadn't left the room long enough for our room to be wired. If the phone had been tapped, we'd barely used it. And we were still on standby, waiting to hear when they were finally leaving

Colombia. If we missed their call, it could blow the whole deal. They weren't going to take off without knowing things were a go here.

"Way I see it, if those *were* cops, they're sure not makin' any moves," I finally said. "I'm gonna go around the side of the hotel, see what's happenin'."

"You're nuts. I'm stayin' put."

I slinked around the side of the building. The moon was high in the sky by then, and I could make out what we thought were cop cars were just junked cars in the salvage yard, the moonlight glinting off the metal and glass.

Back in our room, we laughed at ourselves while having a few drinks, waiting for our nerves to settle down and the speed to wear off enough that we could fall asleep. All night long, I woke up every time there was the slightest noise. That was the last time I took amphetamines.

Late the next morning, we reached Alfredo in Colombia.

"Good," Charlie said into the phone. "Yep"—he looked at the clock—"got it. See you tonight."

He nodded to me as he hung up the phone. "They're all packed and heading over."

I clapped my hands and rubbed them together. "Let's get movin' and shakin'. I hate waiting in these hotel rooms. Especially this one. Don't know whose idea it was to stay in a hotel next to a damn junkyard."

"No shit. I can't wait to see what they got over there this time."

"Don't matter to me. As long as it ain't black beauties." We both cracked up.

Most of the drugs that we smuggled into the country were sold to a connection of Charlie's, a man from California named Bruce. He was ecstatic about our marijuana, saying it was some of the best he'd ever found and consistently high-quality. That kind of reliability made it easy for him to sell. After buying two loads from us, he started buying the pot from us sight unseen. As I expected, he was ecstatic about our cocaine when we could get that. So was I. All of us were. We always took a personal stash of any cocaine we brought into the country.

Bruce had "safe" houses set up all over Miami. The arrangement was simple. We drove a truck or car full of drugs into the garages of these houses and left them there. He then hired older, retired men to drive each vehicle for delivery, usually to California.

This network worked well for us for several months, but Larry kept bugging us to deliver a load to a connection he had in New York, a guy named Dwayne. He talked about Dwayne for a couple of months, but Bruce was so easy we just kept selling to him. Eventually, Larry convinced Alfredo that he could move a much bigger load to Dwayne, way more than Bruce could distribute—like fifteen to twenty thousand pounds. We could each net $200,000 on a load that big. In the end, it was the money we couldn't resist.

But something didn't feel right to me as we put that deal together. For one, I was sure Dwayne was connected to the Mafia, because most of the drugs that moved into New York involved the mob. Even the cops in New York and

New Jersey, a lot of them, were on Mafia payrolls. When I was on the force, those police up there were notorious for being some of the most corrupt in the country. But as long as none of us crossed Dwayne, we'd be fine. Our group always delivered the goods, as promised, so I wasn't worried about that. But as we made plans, things still felt a bit … off.

My first internal warning, that I proceeded to ignore, was that this run required a bigger plane. Dwayne had found a Convair 440 for sale up in Michigan that could easily be retrofitted with extra fuel tanks. Then Ron pointed out that a plane that size required a co-pilot. He'd been flying our DC-3 single-pilot—if he needed a brief assist, he told Alfredo what lever or button to manipulate—but a Convair 440 needed two pilots. Dwayne had a solution to that too, a partner named George, who was a pilot. Ding, ding, ding, ding—warning alarm number two.

We'd been doing just fine with our small group, just the five of us, and our DC-3 bringing in a few tons of marijuana every few months, sometimes a couple dozen kilos of cocaine. We were all making good money, real good money. Larry was making the most, Alfredo next because it was his family's connection, but Charlie, Ron and I were making $100,000 or more on each run. Profit. With what I considered pretty manageable risk. Our arrangement had been working just fine. This new plan introduced two new guys, who no one knew but Larry, two to three times as much marijuana, a different, huge plane and moving stuff through the mob in New York.

Ron looked into the specs for the Convair. When we all met with Dwayne and George, he went over his fuel estimates. "By my calcs, with the extra fuel we'll need and five tons of weed, not six or seven like you've been asking for" —he pointed at Larry—"that's about all a four-forty can get off the ground. In perfect conditions. No headwind, long-ass runway, no trees, no jungle. If we're lucky."

"It'll be fine. Payload's twelve thousand pounds for that Convair," George said, waving his hand at Ron dismissively.

Ron shook his head. "It's ... suicide. For whoever's on that plane." He looked at Alfredo, then at me, Charlie, Larry. "When we started, we all agreed we weren't willing to die for these drugs. What happened to that?"

All eyes were on Ron and George, waiting for them to figure this out, waiting for one of them to convince us that this wasn't a shitty plan, and a suicide mission for Alfredo and the pilots.

"Well, there's no way I'm flying a four-forty with twelve thousand pounds in it. That's crazy," Ron said.

"Done it plenty of times. Just need the right runway."

"Like what, four thousand feet?" Ron asked.

"Minimum."

Ron let out a big exhale. "If we get off the ground in Colombia, if, we'll need a different field here. Like ... almost twice as long as we've been using." He looked at Charlie and me, his lips pressed tight together, shaking his head again. His voice escalated. "And twice as many smudge pots, twice as much time to set it all up, two cargo trucks." He flung his arms out in front of him. "Double everything. All of it."

The room was silent for a few beats. Larry had been staring at the floor. He took a draw off his cigarette.

"Including the money. Double the money." He looked around the room at each of us. "So, who's in?"

Again, the money was what mattered. Double the money. Who could resist? All around the room, including from me, were nods and grunts of "Me," "I'm in," and "Me too."

"But I'll need some time to find another field," I said.

"Plane's gonna cost a hundred thousand bucks. We need half down to hold it," George said. "Then I'll fly it down here a week or so before we go to South America. No sense keepin' it hangared down here until we're ready."

Finally Ron spoke up. "Well, I'm in, but I'm not flying this one."

"We'll need more help at the landing strip, unloading the plane, another cargo truck to drive. I can get a speed roller, but we'll need more manpower here anyways," Charlie said.

"I got another co-pilot I can bring in," George said. He glanced at Dwayne. "Thinkin' of Robert."

Dwayne nodded.

Great. Another new guy. Alarms were going off all over inside my head. Ding, ding, ding, ding.

Over the next few months, while we were working out the details, I invited Larry out for drinks to talk about our new group. "What do you know about Dwayne and these other guy, George and now Robert?"

"Know Dwayne's worked with George for years. George's his main pilot. Don't know anything about Robert, but it's like our group. They all know and trust each other. And I know Dwayne."

"They're Mafia?"

"Let's just say they're close enough to the mob they could reach out and touch them if they wanted to."

That was a lot closer than I cared for. I nodded. "I gotta say, this deal is making me nervous. Three new guys, a new plane, a new field, double the load."

"We're ready. It's time to ramp things up. We can make lots of money on this one. And George and Robert are willing to fly it. Alfredo's all in. What do we have to lose?"

Wasn't much more I could say. Larry was still the moneyman and in charge of this deal. I was either in or out. We'd had several good runs together; no reason not to move forward. Plus, twice as much product meant twice as much money, even with a few more people getting a cut.

"You still in?" Larry asked. "Because you're my man for finding our landing field."

"Oh, I'm in. I found a new field to land in already. About fifty miles south of Orlando. An old pasture field without any cattle on it. I'll scope it out with Robert and George. Ron too, even though he's not flyin', he can help us on the ground with this big-ass runway. It's long, like a damn international runway." We both laughed. "And we have to light it up in a matter of minutes." I shook my head. "Why don't you see if they can get down here sometime in the next month and scope it out. See if it'll work for that Convair."

"Sounds good. We can finalize some of the other details then. I'll reserve a few hotel rooms."

We set the date to meet at the hotel. Ten thousand pounds of marijuana. Charlie, Dwayne, Ron and I'd stay here and prep the landing strip, and Alfredo, Robert and George would fly to Colombia. Larry, of course, wouldn't be risking his life in the air, or getting his shoes muddy in the field. Just fronting over half a million dollars. That's all.

I told Laura the usual, that I'd be out of town for a couple of days on a business trip to South America for gemstones. By this point, she never asked, and I never volunteered any specifics about my "business" trips; those details were best left unspoken between us. Having lots of money reduces stress on a marriage, and Laura was happy being a mom to Julie. Being gone a few days at time, both of us, we hardly saw each other. I was drinking more than ever by then. I could hold lots of liquor, but if Laura came home late and found me passed out on the couch, even if Julie was asleep, man, did that get her hackles up. And I started keeping a little cocaine on hand to keep me from getting too skunked on scotch when I was watching Julie. Worked for me. And it kept me out of trouble with Laura. More and more, we had Laura's parents watch Julie.

There was no moon that night, which was a plus and a minus: harder for anyone to see us but harder for us to see what the hell we were doing. Setting up the smudge pots was slower than I liked, because it was so dark and because laying out a 4,000-foot runway with smudge pots in an old cow pasture was hard work. At one point, I was checking my watch with my lighter and wiping the sweat from my forehead with the back of my hand, when I thought I heard the sound of a car from the direction of the highway.

Charlie jogged over to me. "You hear somethin'?"

"Yeah. Let's get."

We ran across the field to Dwayne and Ron, who, when they saw us come a running, bolted into an orange grove ahead of us. We all came to a stop several rows into the grove. Ron put his hands up to hush us so we could listen. Holding my breath, all I could hear was my pulse thumping in my ears.

We stood motionless for a few minutes, then Dwayne whispered, "Don't think anyone's out there."

"Me neither," Charlie said. "Let's finish settin' things up before they get here."

"Assuming they got off the ground in Colombia," Ron added.

"They got off the ground. Don't worry about that. George knows what he's doin'," Dwayne said.

As we ran back to the field, we heard the faintest whine of a plane engine from the coast. "That's gotta be them," Dwayne said. "I'll radio 'em for more time. We can't get all those smudge pots out and lit in time now. They'll have to circle back around."

As the other three of us hustled to finish setting up the smudge pots, Dwayne started talking into the ground-to-air radio. "Tico Convair, we need ten more minutes. Repeat. We need ten more minutes. Copy?"

Frantic, we shoved the pots into the field, trying to keep the two rows the same distance apart all the way down the line, the sound of the plane's engine growing louder, closer. Then, finally, the engine sound started to move farther away. They got the message. Means we had about ten minutes to finish the landing strip before they circled back.

Dwayne was there now, helping to finish the rows of smudge pots and lighting them. The whine of the engine returned, growing louder and louder. I really couldn't believe they made it.

The last pot was lit. We ran to the edge of the field, in the direction the plane was coming from. All four of us stood, our necks craned, looking up. With all the running lights off, we couldn't see the plane until it roared right overhead and the flames from the pots reflected off the big belly of that beast. Damn, that plane was big: long and twice as tall as our old DC-3. And hopefully full of weed. Excitement and adrenaline was pumping through my body now.

The pasture was much smoother than the sugarcane field we'd used before, so they landed the plane just fine. The four of us ran behind it, extinguishing the smudge pots. As soon as they dropped open the rear cargo door of the Convair, the oily, skunky smell of the pot gushed out. That was some of the strongest-smelling product I'd ever encountered—as a smuggler or a narc. The sheer quantity made the aroma overwhelming, but this smelled like some of the finest, stickiest marijuana Alfredo's connection had ever sold us. Now I was ecstatic. And I didn't even care for smoking pot. But high-quality product meant high profits. We were going to make millions.

I backed one of the cargo trucks up to the open door of the plane. Charlie slid open the truck's loading door and Ron and Dwayne pulled out the speed rollers—aluminum racks like a ladder but with hundreds of metal rollers in between the two parallel rails. I hung my head out the driver's window, waiting to see if I was close enough.

"Back it up. Five more feet," Charlie said. "Little bit more. There, there. Perfect." I jumped out and helped them hoist the ends of two speed rollers up to the floor of the plane where George, Robert and Alfredo were standing. Getting that speed roller balanced wasn't as easy as it sounds, because the floor of the plane was almost as high as the top of the truck. We jiggled the rollers around until they were straight, but the angle was still pretty damn steep.

"Man, don't push those bales out too fast, they're gonna fly into this truck. Right on top of us," Ron said.

We started unloading hundreds of fifty-pound bales of marijuana into the first cargo truck. Robert, George and Alfredo dropped the bales onto the speed rollers and the bales zipped into the trucks super-fast. Each bale was wrapped in black plastic and taped all around, so they were easy to slide around in the truck, but Ron, Charlie, Dwayne and I could barely keep up, shoving the bales forward and stacking them.

Within minutes, I was drenched in sweat, breathing heavy and this nagging, uneasy feeling settled over me. I thought my uneasiness was from the tension of working with these new guys, because we didn't have any comradery with them. But we had serious work to do and fast. Speed was the key to everything. The less time the plane and trucks were sitting in the field, the less time *we* were sitting in the field. When the plane was back in the air and the trucks on the highway, the chance of getting caught dropped significantly. Best time to make an arrest is when all the criminals and the product are all in one place. The more scattered suspects became, the weaker the case.

As the truck filled up, it got harder to move around. "Shit, we're getting buried in here. Slow it down, man," Ron said in a hushed voice up towards the plane.

"Let's just use one roller now. Give us some more room in here," I said. "And someone oughta go scout around the field."

"Why? You hear somethin'?" Charlie asked.

"No, but I can't hear shit in this truck and with speed rollers rattling. That's my point."

"It's a good idea. I'll go," Robert said from up in the plane. "Make sure everything's cool."

Dwayne and I jumped down from the truck and removed one of the rollers from the plane. Outside the truck, I heard the front door of the plane open, then footsteps, Robert walking away from the plane. We'd never had that conversation with the New York crew about who was packing guns and, if so, why. Warning bells again.

Dwayne closed and padlocked the truck loading door. I climbed into the driver's seat. Charlie and Ron would drive the second truck once it was full and after they helped Alfredo light the smudge pots so Robert and George could fly the plane back to the rented hangar at the Ti-Co Airport. Then, those three would extinguish the pots, load them into the pickup, and Alfredo would drive it back to the hotel meeting location. He, George and Robert would need to crash after flying all day from South America.

The other four of us would deliver the trucks to Dwayne's men in North Carolina, get paid, get a rental car and drive back to the hotel meeting location. Dwayne's men would drive the trucks on up to New York. North Carolina was a great state to transport drugs through for two reasons: the halfway point to large metropolitan areas like New York, New Jersey; and North Carolina was full of small towns with dinky sheriff's departments. And some small town in the Carolinas wasn't on the DEA's radar by any means. DEA had its hands full with Miami and New York and Jersey.

Before we pulled away from the plane, I turned the A/C vent to blast at my face. My shirt was soaked with sweat and I reeked of marijuana. I put the truck in gear and it jerked into motion. Finally. Being on the move was always a relief. All that marijuana, some of the finest and worth millions, was safe in my hands, in my control. Yep, we were going to make a killing alright.

I felt supreme as I hung a flashlight out the window so I could keep the truck on the gravel road; no headlights until I hit the paved road. The truck crept along, gravel crunching under the tires. After a slight turn, the road straightened and I picked up a little speed. Not too much, so the engine wasn't making much noise, maybe ten miles per hour. Suddenly, I was blinded—by headlights shining into the windshield of my truck.

CHAPTER 11
JUST A GAME

There I was driving a truck with six tons of weed in it, and next thing I know, I'm squinting into the headlights of a vehicle. I stopped breathing for a few seconds, aware only of my pulse pounding in my ears. Then blue lights started swirling from the top of the car in front of me. As soon as I began to brake, Dwayne jumped out the passenger door. In the seconds all of this happened, I didn't even consider running. I knew what police did when suspects ran, and I wasn't prepared to die that night. Not over a load of drugs, even one worth a million bucks.

I brought my truck to a dead stop face-to-face a few yards from a police cruiser.

I became just a truck driver and started rehearsing in my mind, Hey, I was just hired to drive this truck. But I knew where I was headed—prison. I was hauling three tons of weed down the road. That evidence would be difficult to get out from under.

The deputy had his weapon trained on my windshield.

"Step on outta the truck. Hands up high where I can see 'em." How many times had I said those very words to someone whose heart was pounding in *their* chest? He was doing exactly what he should've been doing given the circumstance: a cargo truck with no lights, middle of the night, creeping along a back road next to an empty field, out there in the boonies. He knew exactly what was going on.

I stepped out, hands high, empty and visible. "Sure thing, officer. My truck battery's dyin' or somethin'. Lost my engine power. All my lights went out."

As he came closer, I could see he was a rookie, maybe in his early twenties—about the age Carl was when he and I started working undercover. He looked like a cowboy in a uniform, what with those wide-brimmed, campaign hats that deputies wore there in ranching country.

Two other patrol cars, lights flashing, pulled up behind the first one, lighting up the fields all arounds us. I'm sure my partners were gone by now. The deputy cuffed me, read me my rights and nudged me in the direction of his vehicle while talking to the other deputies.

As he was opening the back door of his cruiser, when BLAM! A shotgun exploded into the air. It came from the south side of the road. Instantly, Cowboy and I dropped to the ground—well, he dropped, I sort of flopped because my hands were cuffed behind my back. As my shoulder slammed onto road, pain shot down my arm. Chck, chck, BLAM! That one hit the truck.

My brain automatically went into assessment mode. Pump-action shotgun, fired from the south. Not police, not with a shotgun and not in our direction with one of theirs right here and me already cuffed. Dwayne didn't have a shotgun when he bolted from the truck. Must be Robert, probably was still scouting the field when he saw the police lights. He, clearly, wasn't going down without a fight. Hoped he wasn't shooting to kill. Whatever his reason, I didn't much care for the fact that he was shooting in my direction.

Another shot hit the truck, and I listened to it ringing in the air, waiting for another shot. I rolled and scooted as close to the car as I could, my face scraping across the dirt like a damn snake. Wished that rookie would uncuff me, but not likely with live gunfire. If I could've, I would've crawled under that cruiser. After a few seconds, then thirty, then a couple minutes, seemed like the shooting stopped.

I turned my head to one side, then the other, then over my shoulder trying to scan the situation as best I could, given the cuffs and my face planted in the dirt. In the light spinning from the cruiser, I couldn't make out much. Cowboy Deputy was about as far under the car as I was. Being hunkered down there with a cop was almost comical, except we were being shot at. And I wasn't in a uniform any more. I'd be in one soon enough though—a bright orange one at the county jail.

The deputy looked over at me then. "I believe they're tryin' to kill you and me both."

"Sure sounds that way," I said. "Hope they don't get us. Whoever they are." What the hell *are* they doing, I thought. This wasn't part of the deal. My coworkers and I, the five of us, always agreed that if we got caught, that was it. We would just do our time. Nobody ratted anybody else out, and we would never risk getting killed over this shit. I had a family, two of them, to take care of. And one sure way to get killed smuggling drugs is to shoot at the police.

"How many more are out there?" he asked.

"I don't know nothin' about this. I'm a real estate agent and do this, drive trucks"—I ticked my head back towards my truck—"to pick up some extra cash when I can."

By then two more patrol cars pulled alongside us. "What's your status? Anyone hit?"

"No. No one's hit here." The deputy lifted himself off the road, brushed off his hands, picked up his hat. "I've got one suspect here. Unarmed. They're shootin' at the truck mainly. From the south. Right over there." He pointed. "No shots for a couple minutes now."

I rolled onto my side then hoisted myself into a seating position so I could see what was happening. Three of the patrol cars drove around us, headed in the direction of the plane and the other cargo truck. Cowboy Deputy pulled me up by my elbow and, again, led me to the back of his cruiser.

He drilled me with questions, which is exactly what he should've been doing, with officers in hot pursuit of an armed and potentially dangerous suspect. The more information he could feed them, the safer they'd be. He was a pretty good cop. "How many partners you got back there? How many weapons? How many other vehicles back there? Where's the plane? Was everyone else still at the plane when you left? How many are south of the road?"

And I did exactly what I should've been doing, which was keep my damn mouth shut. I shook my head. "Like I said, I just get paid to come out here and drive this truck. I don't ask what's in it. Don't know nothin' about any of this."

A short time later, one of the cruisers returned without anybody in the back. Apparently, they didn't catch anyone else, and I hadn't heard a call for an ambulance over the radio, so no one had been shot. Good. This was just a game, after all. Least by my standards.

No matter what side you were on, sneaking drugs into the country or catching smugglers, we were all playing the same game. Only I stood to earn a whole lot more money on the side I was on now. But none of it was worth killing or dying for.

Only the New York mob guys seemed to be playing a different game.

Over the police radio, I heard that two patrol cars were following vehicle tracks out through the fields north of the plane to the highway, in pursuit of an unknown number of armed fugitives.

As I sat in the back of the cruiser—a place I couldn't actually recall ever being, though I'd shoved many people in there—here's what I figured had happened. As soon as those guys saw the blue lights, Robert started shooting in the direction of the cargo truck and patrol car as a delay-and-distract tactic. There was another scenario playing out in my mind where Robert was actually trying to shoot me because he thought I would rat everyone out.

Robert was always the least interested in getting to know any of us, and the most interested in just getting his cut of the money. I pushed that thought aside for now.

Ruminating on that would only piss me off. What I needed to be right now was calm and cool. And innocent.

Two deputies walked to the trunk, talking and shaking their heads but I couldn't hear what they were saying. They returned with bolt cutters. A lieutenant on the scene was in charge now. He leaned down, head level with the open window. "Understand you agreed we can take a peek at what's in your truck? Cuz it sure smells a lot like marijuana to me. Don't s'pose you got the keys?"

I shook my head.

"Didn't think so."

"Like I said—"

"I know. I know. You're just an innocent truck driver. Well, we're gonna take a look."

"Go right ahead. Like I told the deputy there who cuffed me"—I tipped my chin in Cowboy's direction—"I don't know nothin' about what's in that truck. I'd sure like to know myself, given someone shot at me for it. Think I'll just stick with sellin' real—"

He turned and walked away, bolt cutters dangling from his hand.

I'd heard a lifetime of bullshit like I was now spewing. Just about every suspect I ever arrested had some lame story about why they were innocent. Now I understood how automatic it is, given that anything you say can and will be used against you and so on.

Three of them walked around the back of the truck, out of sight. After several seconds, I heard the clunk of the bolt cutters and the rattle of the door rolling open. I imagined them staring at all those bales stacked floor-to-ceiling, hundreds of them. Imagined the skunky, sweet aroma of that fine product flooding over them. One of them came around front and started searching the truck cab, where they'd find my suitcase, my fake passport and my Browning nine-millimeter. It was definitely all over for me.

Several minutes later, Cowboy walked back to the cruiser with a piece of paper in his hand. He scooched into the front seat and wagged the paper in the air while looking over his shoulder at me. "Is this where y'all were stayin'? The Holiday Inn over at Fort Pierce?"

We'd been staying in a few different hotels in the area so we weren't in one place for too long. Charlie, Ron, Dwayne and I stayed at a hotel in Titusville while Alfredo, Robert and George flew to South America and back. Then tonight, Alfredo, Robert and George had reservations in Melbourne, where they'd wait for us to get back from North Carolina. The night after that, we all had rooms in Fort Pierce, where we'd all settle up with Larry and get our share of the money. My room reservation for tomorrow's hotel was in my wallet, out of habit, I guess. When you're smuggling six tons of weed into the country, landing a Convair 440 in a rancher's field, you don't really worry about a sheet of paper with your hotel reservation on it.

"That's for tomorrow night. Me and my wife were gonna meet up after I finished this job. Got a sailboat we like to rent from the marina there. Do a little fishin', make it a long weekend to celebrate the fourth of July. A little getaway." I gave him a big grin.

He hopped back out and talked to the other deputies by the truck, then one radioed something in. No doubt sending a deputy over to the Fort Pierce hotel. That's okay, none of those guys would be there until tomorrow night.

As I sat in the back of that cruiser for over an hour, I ran this particular deal over and over in my brain trying to determine if I'd been set up by one of my partners and which one. I replayed it all, from the second those headlights beamed into my truck, all the way back to when Larry first suggested we bring a bigger load in from Colombia: all the months of planning, all the phone calls, all the hotels and restaurants and bars we met at to discuss planes and runways and cargo trucks. If one of them had ratted us out, had been an informant this whole time, I'd have known. No one from my original group was an informant; we'd have been arrested already. Course I didn't have a good read on those guys from New York: Dwayne, George and Robert.

Deputy Cowboy came back to the car off and on to fill out paperwork or ask me more questions, so I decided to do a little of my own data collection while I had the chance. If I could keep him talking, I might be able to tell if he was fibbing, covering up for an informant.

"So, what were you doin' out here in the middle of the night? This your regular beat?" I asked.

He paused his scribbling on a clipboard and looked at me in the rearview mirror. "Yeah, I cruise the highway regular and some of the ranchers out here like me to check the side roads once in a while. Used to be they were concerned about cattle thieves, but anymore, they're worried about the low-flyin' aircraft"—he raised his eyebrows—"cuz we all know what that sound means." His slight Southern accent made him seem even more like a cowboy. Probably a nice family man just doing his job. "But tonight, y'all flew right over a deputy's house."

What were the chances a policeman lived right under our flight path? I kept my face neutral, blank, just listening.

"Course he called it in. Orlando Airport had also reported a plane in the area that had just dropped below radar. When I got the BOLO … that means be on the look-out"—didn't seem pertinent for me to tell him that I knew all about BOLOs—"for a plane without any nav lights, I stepped outta my car to listen and y'all flew right over me. *Loowww,* like I coulda reached out and touched the landing gear. I knew you were about to land, so I headed in the direction the plane went."

"You get lots of low-flyin' planes out here then?"

He shook his head. "Nah, but when we do, it's always drugs. I got lucky tonight. Was in the right place at the right time." Then he pointed at me in his mirror. "You, on the other hand, not so lucky."

"Man, you're not kiddin' about that. Seems I was definitely in the wrong place at the wrong time tonight. After this, no more moonlighting as a truck driver for me."

This wasn't part of an undercover op. Just like the Cowboy said, all luck. Tonight, he was a lucky cop, and I was an unlucky smuggler. But I couldn't shake that nagging voice in my head saying, This all sounds too good to be true for the sheriff's department. And how come I'm the only one sittin' in a patrol car right now?

My partners and I'd gotten seven, eight good loads in, made some good money, real good money, and now I'd been caught. I'd say that was a pretty good run. Anyone can smuggle drugs once, make thirty, forty grand, and stop there. That was good money if you'd been making $10,000 a year in your day job. And I knew guys who did that, made one good run, made a killing, then just walked away and invested their money. But I wasn't one of them. Once I made that first run, not the botched one when I was still on the force, but the first one with Alfredo, I was hooked: the easy money, the challenge of planning more and more clever ways to sneak drugs into the country, the exhilaration of succeeding, the reward of Larry handing me a grocery sack stuffed with cash—that's how he paid us because we were way beyond briefcases in terms of the amount of cash we made.

And I was good at smuggling: always kept my head, could read people and knew if they were bullshitting me, could easily spot a narc and knew the tactics they used to try and catch us. I never had a reason to stop, to not make another run, then another and another. I even had Laura fooled, or at least kept the details of my business vague, so she didn't ask many questions or get concerned. She was gone for at least two days twice a week. The way I figured, I'd stop when there was a good reason to stop. Though, I did regret not following my instincts on this deal, but wasn't anything I could do about that now.

I was booked and taken to the Osceola County jail. When I called Laura, she was speechless. I could just imagine the shocked look on her face.

"What on earth happened? Why are you in jail?"

"It's a long story, and I can't get into it all right now. I think I may have taken a fall for somebody, but I'm not sure—"

Julie was in the background asking to talk to me.

"Not right now, sweetheart. Mama needs to talk to

Daddy right now. What's going to happen? When will you get out?"

"There'll be an arraignment and bond hearing, hopefully in a day or two, so I can get out on bail. Then the trial will be set for some time in the near future, but I'll need—"

"What do I need to do? Do I have to post bail for you?"

"No, you don't have to do anything yet. I've got an attorney, Michael Newman, he'll handle everything." Larry always said he had a hotshot attorney who could represent any of us if we were ever caught, and I imagined he would cover all the expenses, too; extra insurance that I wouldn't spill my guts about him running the show for our smuggling ring. No doubt the DEA would pressure me to snitch about who the big guns were in this operation. "All you need to do is talk to Michael when he calls you. He'll tell you everything you need to do. Just do whatever he says."

"Do you need anything? Should I come up—"

"No. Absolutely not. I don't want you up here. I'll be meeting with Michael soon, and I'll ask him to call you and explain what's gonna happen and when. You just stay put for now, take care of Julie and don't worry about this. I'll take care of it."

"You know I'm *going* to worry. How could I not?" I heard a little sob over the phone. "Of course, I am. My husband's in jail. Shouldn't I come up for the … whatever it's called … the first hearing?"

"Just sit tight. The attorney will tell you if and when you should come up. Definitely don't want you up until I can leave with you. Don't you have a flight this week?"

"I'm not flying. Not now. I'll get someone to cover my flight. I want to be here, or there, when you get out."

"Don't bring Julie."

"No, I won't. I'll have my mama watch her."

"I'll be out before you know it. Promise. My time's up here on the phone so I gotta go. You need anything?"

She let out a long sigh. "No. We're fine. Just take care of yourself in there. Is it dangerous, in case someone finds out you were a policeman?"

"Nobody'll know that. And I won't be here for long. Love you darlin'."

"I love you too. You're sure you don't need anything?"

"Not a thing. Give Julie a big hug and kiss for me." That got her going, crying. I hated when women cried, because I never knew what to do to ... well ... to make them stop. "I'll be home before you know it. Trust me. It's all gonna work out fine."

Michael showed up the next day to meet with me. He didn't even look thirty years old, right out of law school and pretty green, but he seemed super-smart and got right to the point. The prosecution had a pretty good case against me, since I was caught red-handed with three tons of marijuana. He would work every angle and, if I was convicted, we would appeal. If that didn't work, he said I'd likely be looking at several years in prison. That's when I decided to tell him about my past life as a cop to impress upon him the importance that I not go to prison, and if I did, hopefully to a low-security prison where I'd be less likely to get whacked. And I asked him to assure me that none of this would be shared with Larry, even if he was paying Michael's fees.

Then he explained that an arraignment would be held

the following week, at which my associates and I would plead not guilty and be released on bond.

"My associates?"

He flipped through police reports, described how five men—he named everyone except Alfredo—had been arrested at the hotel in Melbourne. While he continued to talk, this information was whirring through my brain. That Holiday Inn was in Brevard County, so they would've been booked in the Titusville jail. Explained why they weren't in here with me. But what didn't make any sense was that the hotel reservation was for the place in Fort Pierce, not the one in Melbourne. So, how did the police find them at the Melbourne hotel? And why the hell did they go back to the hotel after I'd been nabbed? Alfredo was probably scared shitless and split. He had the right idea to get as far away from the scene as possible, but that made me suspicious. I thought about my undercover work and how far we went to protect our informants, making arrests when they weren't present.

"Evidence is pretty weak against the others," Michael said. "So the prosecutor's going to ask you to testify against them. Likely shorten your sentence if you—"

"I don't play that game."

For the next few days, I sat in my cell—twelve feet by twelve feet with two metal bunk beds, a metal sink, toilet and a table and chair all bolted to the walls and floors—and ran through my mind what had happened and what I should've done differently. And what exactly I'd do if I found out I'd been set up. Hiring someone to blow up their next plane came to mind several times.

There was no way Alfredo was an informant. DEA was

making inroads into Colombia, but I'd seen Alfredo in Colombia. He wasn't a friend of so-and-so's cousin in South America. Those were clearly his close family members, brothers, brothers-in-law, supplying us with our product. And he wasn't about to risk ratting out his own family.

What about Charlie, I thought. He'd been an informant years earlier, though not a very good one. He was always worried about other dealers finding out he was an informant, and stressed by agents pressuring him to rat on other dealers. Eventually, he just stopped dealing altogether, so he didn't have any new information for the agents. And kept his nose clean so the police didn't have anything new to hold over his head. That spoke volumes to me about his principles—he chose to stop dealing rather than continue snitching. That's one of the reasons I brought him into our group a couple of years earlier: he hated working for cops and valued his reputation on the streets. Plus, he was so transparent. I'd have noticed his anxiety if he was informing again.

And Ron, he'd been our only pilot for close to two years by then. Sure, he got a share of the money for flying, but he wasn't selling a few pounds of marijuana on the side. A person had to get arrested to end up being coerced into become an informant. He just wanted to fly, get paid his share and go home to his wife and kids.

Unless I was losing my instincts, none of the regulars in my group was an informant. Any snitch in our group had to be one of the mob. If someone had snitched, I'd figure out who soon enough. As soon as I was released from this pit of a jail.

The jail was filled to capacity, even with only a few

dozen inmates. With little room to let us move around more freely, we had to remain in our cells except once a day to shower and three times a day for meals. There was another man in my cell, but I kept to myself. Having been a narcotics agent only six years earlier, the less any of these inmates knew about me, the better.

CHAPTER 12
NOT THAT KINDA GAME

Our arraignment took place a week later, and I was released on a $20,000 bond—without my shoes. To place me at the plane, the prosecution needed to match the soil on my shoes with the soil around the plane, so my shoes were now evidence. Those were good shoes too, Sperry Top-Siders. When I'd been on that dynamite crew years earlier, a forklift ran over my foot. Ever since then, most shoes made that foot ache. Except those Top-Siders. The first thing Laura and I did was go shopping for some new shoes. I was barefoot. I bought a new pair of Top-Siders, not the slip-on type, but the type that go higher around your ankle and have shoelaces and a solid rubber sole with good traction. This pair was made with elk leather. So I ended up with an even better pair of work shoes, better for trudging through fields and running when I needed to. I had no intention of quitting work.

After my release, I told Laura the gist of what had happened. She'd hear all the details at the trial, because my attorney said it was a good idea for her to be in the courtroom. It would show that I lived a respectable life, had a professional wife and that I wasn't hustling drugs to kids on street corners. When I told her the story, I downplayed the scale of our operations and for how long I'd been smuggling, assuring her my involvement in that line of work was all over now, that I'd learned my lesson. Just wanted to get the trial over and get all this behind us. In the meantime, I promised her I'd find a legitimate job. Clearly, she wanted to believe me, but I'm not sure she did.

I didn't even look for a job; what a waste of time that would be. I needed to keep smuggling while waiting for my trial. My group lost a lot of money on that deal, over a million bucks. Gone. Me alone, I stood to make at least a $200,000 on that deal. I had to recoup some of that money and couldn't do it selling used cars. Trials took several months, years if we had to appeal. Quitting now made no sense. I needed more money than ever in case my attorney couldn't get me off, and I went to prison. Money to help me finally get a business going when I got back out. And some to set aside for Laura and Julie, and for Linda and the kids.

I hadn't paid child support to Linda in several months, not for lack of money. But the few times I gave her a wad of cash, she got suspicious. Just what a smuggler needs: an angry, suspicious ex-wife. And by then, she'd moved the kids up to Ohio. Couldn't exactly mail her a stack of hundreds. And running my smuggling money through our checking account, and Laura asking about all the money, just so I could mail a child-support check, wasn't an option. So I did what I was really good at by then: put my walls up, avoided child support, avoided ex-wife.

For a couple of weeks after getting out on bail, I laid

low, didn't call Charlie, Alfredo, Larry or Ron, didn't frequent any of our haunts. Then I started hanging out in the bar where I expected to run into one of them eventually. Within a few days, Larry and I were sitting in a back booth having drinks and discussing what had gone down.

"We've worked together for a couple of years now," I said. "A couple of good years, right?"

He nodded.

"Had a real good thing goin'. And I'd like to continue our business if we can. But I have to know what went down last month. Seems to me like we got set up."

Music started pounding through the wall that separated the dance floor from the back part of the lounge where we were talking. Larry leaned forward so he could be heard over the music. "I don't think so, because everyone got arrested. But you know, they all think *you* ratted *them* out. At least Dwayne does. They think you told the pigs where they were staying."

My stomach was on fire despite the antacid I chewed right before I went into the bar. And the scotch wasn't helping either. I needed to keep Larry's confidence. He was the moneyman, the boss, and this was my job. I looked him right in the eyes. "You know I don't work that way. Cops caught me"—I pointed at my chest—"sittin' on a truckload of product. I didn't even know they'd been arrested until Michael told me. But I sure as hell didn't say a word about anyone else. And never will. The cops did find my Fort Pierce hotel reservation for the next night in my wallet."

He stared at me for a few seconds. "You bullshitting?"

I shook my head and lit a cigarette.

"Why'd you put the paperwork in your—"

"Didn't plan on gettin' arrested." I tossed my hands in the air. "It wasn't for the Melbourne hotel where they got arrested anyways. It was for our meet-up hotel. Why'd they go back to the hotel?"

He shook his head. "Beats me. But man … you need to talk to Dwayne and his pilots. Get them straight on this before they go trashing your reputation, telling people you're a snitch."

"Oh, I'm lookin' forward to talking with them. I'd like to know why the hell they shot at me with a pump-action shotgun. We all need to get this straightened out. Before the trial starts."

"I don't know any of the details and don't want to. I wasn't there. All I know is I lost a shit-ton of money on this one." He tapped his index finger on the table between us. "A lot."

"And I plan to pay you back for every penny of my share of that loss. I don't wanna bring any heat to anyone, but I'd like to keep doing my part, earn that money back for you. You know I'm good for it. And if I have to pay you back selling real estate, it's gonna take about ten years."

We both laughed.

"Trial's not set yet, but Michael expects it'll be early next year. If they convict, we'll appeal. So, I got a year, maybe two. Plenty of time to pay you back. I'd love to keep doin' business with you."

He pursed his lips, thinking. I took a sip of my scotch and waited. I couldn't get things going with a new group right now; it had to be with my old group, the guys I knew I could rely on. But if Larry insisted on keeping Dwayne and his men on with us, then I was out.

I took another sip of scotch, then said, "I prefer we go back to Bruce and our DC-3, now that the Convair's gone. Bruce is a sure deal, working with him's predictable. It'll take a bit longer to make the money back, cuz we'll bring in smaller loads. But we wouldn't need Dwayne and his pilots, so fewer men, bit more manageable." I crushed my cigarette in the ashtray. "Course, it's up to you."

Larry tossed back the rest of his drink, then stared down into his glass, rattling the ice cubes around. "Okay. You talk to the others and see if they're up for it. There's plenty more work to do, that's for sure. Alfredo says he can have another delivery in a month or two."

I couldn't stop the smile from spreading across my face. A month was even sooner than I'd hoped. Looked like I was back in business.

Larry and I spent another hour reaching an agreement about our new working relationship. As long as I stayed involved, financially and otherwise, and kept my mouth shut, I'd get paid for my part. I wouldn't earn as much as I'd been getting on each run. The less involved you were, the less risk you assumed, the less money you made. But it was better than selling real estate. Larry even offered to let me and my family stay, rent-free, in one of several houses.

Larry would keep his distance from me but pay me well. I wouldn't turn state's evidence against him; I'm not a snitch. And I like to think Larry knew that about me, but I'm sure he felt a whole lot more confident keeping me on the payroll and taking care of all my trial expenses. It was insurance that I wouldn't implicate him in any way during the trial. Trust only goes so far when someone's taking a fall for someone else, especially when that person is staring at prison time.

During my first meeting with Charlie, Ron and Alfredo to discuss making another run, we all talked about the arrest first.

Ron started off. "As soon as we saw that pig's lights, George grabbed his bag from the plane and pulled out a shotgun. Told us to load up in the truck, he'd be right back. Right then Robert ran up, then Dwayne. I asked where you were, and he said, 'I don't know. I split.' We were all piling into the pickup when the shotgun started going off. I figured George was trying to make the pigs think we were over in his direction, slow them down so we could make a run for it."

"I jumped in the driver's seat," said Charlie. "Everyone else climbed in and George was the last in. He jumped into the bed of the truck and said, 'Go! Go!' We asked if he'd seen you, but he said he couldn't see shit out there. I peeled outta there, headed straight to the highway. Right through the fields." He shook his head. "Plowed right through some fences. Good thing there were no cows out there. We would've never made it to the highway in one piece."

"Why'd you go back to the hotel?"

"It's where our stuff was, our cars. We thought switching vehicles would be better than driving around in that truck. And all of our stuff, evidence, was still in the rooms."

"I had nothing in the room," Alfredo said, shaking his

head. "I put all in my car before we fly to Colombia. I was not going back into hotel."

"I was sure no one followed us, cuz it was pitch black until I bounced outta that field and hit the highway. Figured we were home free," Charlie said.

"Well, they weren't too far behind us, cuz me and Dwayne were grabbing our stuff when they pounded on the door," Ron said. "We knew we were fucked. DEA officers started harassing us about the smell of hydraulic fuel and pot in the room, on our clothes, asking if we'd just left our plane. I told them I was a diesel mechanic, just got off a long shift at work, went out for a few drinks, hadn't had a chance to get showered up yet. They didn't buy it, obviously. Wanted to know if I had an alibi from work or from the bar, on and on. By the time they cuffed us, I saw another cop hauling you guys from the other room." He pointed at Charlie.

"Same kinda shit in our room," Charlie said, chuckling. "Only we told the pigs our boat motor broke and—"

"Would've been a big boat motor to make you to reek *that* bad," Ron said. "Those auxiliary fuel tanks in the plane were a mess ..." He shook his head.

Charlie shrugged. "I told 'em we'd been stuck out on the water trying to get that motor running for hours. Finally got hauled in by another boat. Course they wanted to know who hauled us to shore. I said, 'I didn't ask their names, just thanked 'em.' Offered to show where they moored their boat, maybe find the owners to prove our alibi. The cop said that'd be tough, since we were goin' to jail."

"Attorney says unless DEA can come up with some solid evidence that puts us at the plane with the weed, we'll likely be acquitted. So, you"—Ron shook the cigarette that was burning between his fingers at me—"better keep your mouth shut."

I waved his comment away. "You know me better 'an that. I won't say shit to the DEA. What about you guys? You'll keep your traps shut? We're all in agreement. No one rats on anyone here?"

Nods and "Of course," from Ron and Charlie.

A couple of weeks later, I met up with Dwayne and George for drinks when they were in Miami.

"I'm just gonna lay it all out here. I didn't tell the cops anything about you or the hotel we stayed in. Nothin'. And I won't. They found my reservation for the Fort Pierce hotel, not the one where you got busted. So I don't know how they found you all in Melbourne."

"Who keeps a damn reservation when they're smuggling?" George said.

"Who the hell shoots at his partner, that's what I'd like to know. Why the hell'd you shoot at me? A couple of those shots came pretty damn close."

"It was darker 'an shit out there," George said. "I couldn't see a thing but the shape of the truck. Figured the truck was safe to hit and close enough to slow 'em down. Wanted to give us some time to get the hell outta there. Would've worked if they hadn't found us in the hotel."

"Pfft. Sure seemed like you were shootin' to kill. It's just luck I'm still here. A shotgun, in the dark, towards a police car and the truck I was in. And Dwayne."

"I was long gone by then," Dwayne said.

I pointed at George. "He didn't know that."

Dwayne looked at George, while George stared me down.

I locked eyes with George for a few beats. "That's not the kind of game I play. I don't kill cops—or anyone else—for drugs."

"Wasn't tryin' to kill anyone. Just wasn't goin' to prison if I could help it."

Definitely Mafia. Those mob guys could care less if they killed me, one of their own, a cop, several cops. Trigger-happy sons of bitches. Swore right then I'd never work with the mob again if I could help it.

CHAPTER 13
SWARMING WITH SMUGGLERS

Before our January arraignment, my original group was able to put one deal together, which required some serious finagling on my part to pull off right under Laura's nose. I'd been doing that all along, but now that my cover had been blown, it was more difficult. But I didn't stay at the hotel or prep the runway, just helped with all the planning, then drove a truck to one of Bruce's safe houses. All things I could do while out "selling real estate." I made about $30,000—I'd definitely moved a few rungs down the ladder. Most of that money I contributed to buying the next load, so I could get a larger return.

Four months after my arrest, Laura and I sold our house and moved into Larry's house. This new housing arrangement had required another bit of finagling on my part to get Laura to agree. My explanation was: the profit from the sale of our house would pay off my bail bond, rent was cheaper than our mortgage and we could sock away more money in case I had to take a long vacation (sounded better than "going to prison," especially if Julie was in earshot). All of this was basically true. Except for the part about paying rent. And about my real estate job. And, I coaxed Laura, the house had five bedrooms so we'd have room for Rick and Lynn to visit.

I did think about those two all the time and was always trying to hold a place for them in my life. Course, they didn't know that because I wasn't very good on the follow-through, on actually bringing them into my life. But here's where my main focus was: I was smuggling large quantities of drugs into the country while hiding it from Laura, the DEA and the U.S. Attorney's Office that was actively building a felony case against me. So adding into the mix an ex-wife and two teenagers I had to fly down from Ohio really complicated matters.

Rick wasn't interested in visiting me by then anyways. Linda had called me a few times, all upset about the trouble he was into: truant at high school, drinking, doing drugs. On one of those calls she mentioned Lynn seemed to be following in Rick's footsteps. All problems I was in no position to help with.

The only time I was of much help was right before they all moved up to Ohio the year before. Linda had the house sold, everything packed and ready to relocate, when Rick got arrested shoplifting. I paid an attorney to handle the case. He arranged for Rick to serve probation in Ohio, so they didn't have to wait around for weeks in Miami awaiting a trial. Arrests and attorneys—now that was the kind of trouble I could help with. But trying to help an ex-wife with teenagers who were using drugs? I was working on concealing my *own* drug use from Laura.

It was 1980, and Colombian cocaine was flooding into

the country, mostly through Miami. We were right there in the thick of it. And a lot of that blow was going right up my nose. Cocaine lit me up and made me feel so alive, especially the pure stuff. It made my thinking more clear, especially if we were on a run that had me up for days.

When I had a stash of coke, I drank less. Laura had asked me, many times, to cut down on my drinking, especially when I was watching Julie, which was a few days a week. With cocaine, it was less obvious that I was high. So, I snorted more, drank less. I don't think Laura suspected I was using drugs. Not at first.

It looked like the DEA and the U.S. Attorney had pretty solid evidence to convict me but weak evidence against the five others that were arrested at the hotel. The prosecution had no evidence they'd been at the plane and none of them had any marijuana on them when they were arrested. Everyone knew they were guilty, but that didn't matter. The prosecutor had no proof. I'd always hated those cases when I was undercover: watching guilty people walk. That's why the where and how of the arrests were always so critical. I was going to hate this too, watching my partners walk when I was looking at prison time. Unless this attorney was as good as Larry said.

While the prosecution was preparing a case against us, they offered to reduce the charges against me if I turned state's evidence and testified who I was working with, and for. We all knew they would plea-bargain with me. If I didn't testify against the others who were involved, the prosecutors didn't have shit on them. Prosecution knew it. I knew it. My partners most definitely knew it. Part of the DEA's mission was to work their way up the ladder to the ones who were running the show, the moneymen. In this case, that was Larry. But I didn't play that kind of game. My game was getting the stuff into the country without getting popped. On that particular hand, I lost. But there was no reason to bring somebody else down with me.

Our trial was held in Orlando nine months after I'd been arrested and lasted several days. The first day I walked into the courtroom, I scanned the room—the judge, the jurors, the prosecuting attorney, the DEA special agent who investigated the case, all of our attorneys (we all had our own by then; I just stuck with Michael, Larry's attorney) and the deputies who arrested us. I figured the prosecutor and the DEA agent, whose name sounded familiar to me, knew by then that I used to be a narcotics agent. That was a little rough, knowing they were judging me, thinking, knowing I'd sold out, given in to the temptation. But God knows I wasn't the first cop to end up on the other side by then.

But I blocked all that out, flipped my internal switch and my walls went up. The Cowboy Deputy who'd arrested me was there and testified. The usual stuff. Yes, I was the man driving the truck. No, I didn't try to flee. Yes, the truck I was driving was full of bales of marijuana. No, I didn't resist arrest. Yes, I cooperated with the deputies. Nothing too exciting for him today, not compared to us hiding under his patrol car while George shot at us.

All the evidence was there: dozens of photos of the plane, the cargo trucks and the bales of marijuana; my shoes with dirt on them, of course the same dirt found around the plane; that God-damn hotel reservation; my fake passport; my Marlboros with fingerprints; and my Browning nine-millimeter. Boy, I hated to lose that gun. I had it since I was an agent. There on that evidence table I could see, plain as day, the most likely outcome of the trial. While I held a shred of hope that Michael might, somehow, get me off, I was resigned to the fact that I was going to prison. If he was any good, he'd at least get me a short sentence.

Every day I showed up at court and went through the motions, trying to look remorseful and repentant, slipping Rolaids in my mouth and counting the hours until I could take that tie off and sip a scotch by the hotel pool.

The jury found me guilty on two felony counts: conspiracy to possess marijuana and possession of marijuana with an intent to distribute. Such funny wording. What the hell else would you do with six tons of marijuana? You bet I intended to distribute it. Had intended to get paid a lot of money for those six tons too.

The other five men were acquitted, had charges against them dismissed because there wasn't enough evidence or had their cases declared mistrials.

Sentencing happened the following week. I was given four years for each felony count. My attorney filed an appeal right away. Winning would be a longshot, but an appeal gave me more time. More time to be free. More time to earn some of that money back.

Things really heated up between Laura and me after the trial—and I don't mean the sex. She saw the writing on the wall, knew I was likely going to prison. Hearing some of the nitty-gritty details of our operations, and seeing all that evidence, probably wasn't easy for her. With her eyes now wide open, I couldn't very well hide my smuggling from her. And I was snorting cocaine regularly, in increasing amounts, and getting lazy about hiding my stash.

The longer you're in that drug world, the more that lifestyle takes over you, just like working as an undercover agent. Once again, I was trying to keep my two worlds from colliding, but they were bumping against each other. Regularly.

Once, instead of making a delivery, I told a connection to come to my home and pick up the drugs, because I had Julie and didn't want to haul her into a potentially dangerous situation. The way I saw it, my house was a controlled environment. But there I was crossing those lines again, those lines between my two worlds.

Another time, Laura came home to find me snockered, passed out, on the couch. Luckily, Julie was already in bed. I'd been on a run for the past forty-eight hours while Laura was on a flight. Laura's parents had kept Julie the night before, since I was also gone on business. By the time Laura got home, I hadn't slept in over twenty-four hours and had several scotches that day. Not to mention the coke I'd been snorting for two days. She was livid by the time I finally came to.

Laura began to press me about the house we were living in, questioning if it belonged to Larry, who she'd learned about during the trial. "This house belongs to that man who paid for all that drug dealing, doesn't it? He's your boss or whatever you call it?"

"I told you, it belongs to a friend of mine. He's just tryin' to help—"

"John, I'm not stupid. You're still at it with the drugs. I know it. I just can't do this. We have a child. We can't have her around this"—she lifted her arms out to her sides then dropped them, her hands slapping against her thighs— "craziness. It's dangerous."

"Darlin', listen to me. I'm not involved in anything dangerous. You've gotta know that. I wouldn't put you or Julie in any kind of danger. Never. I just wouldn't do that."

"That man was shooting at that truck. I heard the officers in the hearing. These are dangerous people." She stared at me. "I can't live this way anymore. I love you. I want to be with you. But I won't live this way. We have a daughter. She's my priority ... and should be yours."

She insisted I stay away from the drugs and that we move out of Larry's house. That, or she and Julie would find another place without me. I had plenty of money by then, so we bought our own house just a few miles south of the one we'd been living in. It wasn't as big as Larry's but was twice the size of the little house we'd bought when we'd first moved back to Miami. At least I wasn't moving backwards. Laura and Julie would be comfortable in the house, and I wouldn't have wanted them staying in Larry's house if I ended up in prison.

My appeal didn't take place for another year, during which time I was involved in five or six more deals, always cocaine. I rode that train for as long as I could: worked as many deals as possible, snorted as much as I could get away with and raked in the money. Finally, that easy money was coming my way. I was swamped in money. Big grocery bags full of cash.

I know smuggling while awaiting an appeal sounds

risky, some would say insane. But I was watching my back, vigilant that I didn't bring any heat to me or anyone in my group. But I really wasn't worried about being watched by the DEA. The Feds were way too busy to keep track of me. Miami was swarming with smugglers by then.

CHAPTER 14
A LONG VACATION

My appeal was denied, and I was given four days to report to the federal penitentiary at Eglin Air Force Base. As much as I hated to, I called Linda and told her the gist of what happened. Better than just disappearing—well, completely disappearing this time. Didn't want her to think I was dead, though I'm sure she'd wished *that* a few times over the past few years. That was actually one of the toughest conversations I had before reporting to prison, because she was one of the few people in the world who knew me when I was at my absolute best, at my peak. And here I was, at my worst, the lowest. She wanted to know what and when I was planning to tell the kids.

Now that was a conversation I definitely didn't want to have. Julie was too young to understand what was happening, she was only five, but Lynn and Rick were like, fourteen and seventeen. It'd be such a bad influence for them to know I was a drug smuggler and all. I promised Linda I'd write the kids a letter and explain everything, but I never did. I just didn't have the guts, not because I was ashamed, more that I … hated to let my kids down. What I'd done was illegal, but I still had my principles. But they wouldn't have understood the value of me not ratting out my partners just to get a lighter sentence, or never hurting anyone, or not selling drugs to high-school kids. Eventually, so much time had passed that I figured Linda had already told them, so I didn't bother trying. Another one of those decisions that I let life make for me.

Called my folks to tell them I'd be gone for a few years —overseas on a special undercover assignment—and that I'd call them every month or so. Mom said the usual, that she'd pray for me, but Dad didn't say much. Pretty sure he knew something was wrong.

Laura wanted to make plans for her to come up and visit me, without Julie, but I wasn't sure I wanted her up there. Partly because I didn't want her to see me incarcerated. It was degrading, being in prison with no way to provide for Laura or entertain her or romance her. Plus, with no freedom to speak of in the future, seeing her would just make me feel worse. I didn't want to feel any of that shit while I was in prison. You've got to stay tough, hard in prison, even a minimum-security one. Definitely didn't want to be moping around every week, hoping she'd visit. I just told her to wait and see how I felt once I got settled in the pen.

My last night as a free man, Laura, Julie and I went out for a fancy dinner. Escargot appetizer, medium-rare prime rib and a loaded baked potato for me. "And don't let this dry up," I told our waitress, tapping on my first scotch, one ice cube. The waitress prepared our dessert tableside, flaming the sugar to a crackling caramel topping on crème brûlée.

Back at home, I tucked Julie in and read her a bedtime story. It occurred to me that when I got out, she'd be twice the age she was right then; half her life will have passed without me around. She might not even remember me.

Then Laura and I went straight to bed. She was sad, to say the least, but I wasn't wasting my last night moping around—that could be my last chance for sex for years. When we finally went to sleep, I slept through the night, like I didn't have a care in the world.

The next day, I was to report to the Eglin Prison Camp before five p.m. or a warrant would be issued for my arrest. I didn't want Laura saying good-bye to me there. Better at home. So, Charlie picked me up at six a.m. It was nine-hour drive to Eglin. We snorted coke the whole way.

There were several hundred inmates at Eglin. While we had a structured schedule and had to work full-time, we could move freely around the compound. Because it was a low-security penitentiary, there were no barbed-wire fences or walls; just a painted line that inmates were not allowed to cross. Some prisoners, depending on their crime and their behavior in the pen, could eventually earn privileges to visit with family at a nearby motel. Now if I could earn those privileges, I'd let Laura visit me. But until then, I didn't want Laura visiting me. Not at the prison. I didn't want her stepping foot in there. She was too classy for that.

The buildings were former barracks on an unused portion of Eglin Air Force Base. Each barrack was divided into a couple dozen two-man cubicles. The guards took head counts every four hours. If an inmate tried to escape, his sentence would be lengthened or he would be sent to a higher-security prison. No one bothered. We all knew we were lucky to be at that pen.

Prison life wasn't that much different from military life: being accountable to someone higher up the ladder than you are; having a regimented schedule for waking, eating, working, sleeping, for everything; being surrounded mostly by men. Being imprisoned on an active military base was also familiar. Hearing jets ripping off the runway or screaming through the air, seeing men in their camouflaged uniforms or watching troops perform maneuvers, all of it triggered deep memories, almost physical ones, of being in the Marines. I could almost smell the petroleum of the shoe polish I'd used to bring my combat boots to a shine, feel the stiff creases in my dress blues, hear the laughter among the men in my platoon.

What I *didn't* feel at Eglin Air Force Base was how alive I felt, how full of promise my life was when I was a Marine. That part was definitely missing.

And the scotch. The scotch was missing. I was surprised how much I craved a drink. Without any booze for me to use to become someone else, to escape from myself, there I was. Without the scotch to help me see life the way I wanted to see it, I saw my life in stark clarity. Every day, I faced what had become of my life. My life seemed unreal, like I'd taken a ten-year detour. A really long, bad detour.

The slow pace of prison life was tough to adjust to. The smuggling life, especially when cocaine-fueled, is anything but slow and predictable.

I sure didn't expect to be so lonely either. After a month, I decided to call my father.

"Hey Dad. How are you and Mom doing?" I tried to sound upbeat.

"We're fine. Just fine. I'm glad you called, because I've had a real bad feeling about you since we last spoke."

"About what? Everything's great here. I'm just—"

"You're in trouble, aren't you?"

The last thing I needed on top of hating my life and disappointing Laura, was to let my folks down, especially with Dad's history of really bad heart attacks, and Mom, well, she was such a worrier. I let out a sigh. "To be honest with you, Pop, I've gotten into some trouble. But I really don't want you all worrying. And I don't want Mom to know. She'll just—"

"You let me make that decision, whether to tell her. Her faith is stronger than you think. Why don't you start by telling me what's going on."

"Well … I got messed up in some bad business after I left the force and ended up"—another inmate walked up to the phone to my left, so I turned away, facing the phone on the right that wasn't being used—"taking a fall for someone."

"So, where are you?"

"In prison … down here in Florida." I thought about explaining that it was a low-security pen, but that didn't matter, not to him. Prison was prison, bars or not. I remembered the day I'd graduated from the police academy—at the top of my class. Mom and Dad came down for the graduation. I'd even arranged with the department for Dad to pin my badge on during the cere-mony. I wasn't sure who was prouder that day, me or him.

"Are you still there?" His words snapped me back to the murmur of other prisoners talking around me.

"Yeah, I'm here."

"How long will you be there?"

"About four years. But I plan to get out early for good behavior." The phone line hummed.

"What can I do? What do you need?"

"Nothin'. I'll call you every now and again. It's just good to talk."

"You call whenever you can … whenever you want. And I'll be praying for you. You know, God will forgive—"

"I know. I know. Believe me, I been praying a lot lately."

As I hung up the phone, I wondered how the hell a preacher's son ended up here.

CHAPTER 15
THE STRAIGHT AND NARROW

Being the son of preacher had colored my childhood in every way. As a young child, I accepted our religion as part of our life, no choice in that matter. We were Reverend Walker's family. For the most part, I believed what I'd been taught.

In my teenage years, I tried to hold onto that religion, but my faith slipped through my fingers like water. Looking back, that's actually the first time I led a double life—the external me and the internal me. I attended Sunday school and church (that's all we were allowed to do on the Sabbath, except eat), was baptized as a teenager (no baby baptism in our church, believers only, full immersion, three dunks) and treated adults with respect. Behind the scenes, I snuck around, smoked, drank and chased girls, even on the Sabbath, when I could get away with it.

Didn't even graduate from high school because me and my best friends developed what we thought was a cherry bomb, so we could leave high school with a little bang, something our classmates would remember.

We'd driven to the high school late that morning, arriving after everyone was already in class. Huddling just inside the front doors, Jay whispered, "You got the bomb?"

I pulled the cherry bomb out from under my jacket. The evening before, we'd added gunpowder and a bigger fuse to a harmless smoke bomb. "Yeah, you guys watch for anyone in the hall while I light it." I set the bomb at the base of the front doors, struck a match and waited until the fuse began to hiss. "Go, go, go," I said and we skittered down the hallway, snickering.

When I heard how loud the explosion was, my heart sank with the thought of how disappointed my parents were going to be. My father was a patient man, but he could be stern. And my mother, she was just … devout. Her solution to everything was to pray, though her prayers didn't seem to work because she never stopped fretting and worrying.

The school door was blasted clear off its hinges. We had no idea our little bomb would do so much damage. The three of us were expelled from high school two weeks before graduation.

The military had seemed like my best option after that, so I went down to the Armed Services recruiting office and enlisted in the Marines. My parents were pacifists by Brethren Church doctrine, didn't believe in war or even military participation. They were disappointed, to say the least. Me joining the Marine Corps was a rejection of my upbringing. Pop tried to talk me out of joining, but it was too late. I'd already signed up for four years. Man, had I been excited to get out of that little town in the-middle-of-nowhere Ohio.

After my four years in the Marines was up, Linda and I moved to Indiana, where I attended seminary college. Just following my father's footsteps and my mom's wishes, I guess. After the Marines and living in Hawaii, seminary classes and Indiana weren't too exciting (imagine that?), even if my parents were happy I'd enrolled. Lynn had been born by then, so we had two babies. I was taking college classes, working part-time and trying to help out with the babies. Here I was, twenty-four-years old, and my wife was supporting us with her nursing job. Man, I hated that. Back then, men worked and women stayed home with the kids. I needed a job.

What I really wanted to do was become a pilot and live by the ocean again. Hawaii was way too expensive, so I talked Linda into moving to Miami.

When we first got there, I felt like I was going backwards in life. Living in a cramped apartment was fine when we were twenty and that apartment was walking distance to the beach in Hawaii. But we were twenty-five, and the rundown house we rented was a few miles from one of the worst ghettos in Miami.

We called that the cockroach house (though I realized later that all houses in Miami eventually had cockroaches). If I went into the kitchen at night and flicked the lights on, they'd be crawling all over the walls and counters, even on the ceiling, skittering for cover behind and under the appliances and cupboards. Big, crunchy-looking things. Got so used to them, one scurried up the wall while we were eating breakfast, and I just reached over and smashed it. Bad idea with two toddlers at the table.

To make matters worse than living in a cockroach house

at the edge of the ghetto, pilots were coming back from Vietnam with lots of flying hours. This made it impossible for me, with zero hours, to get hired and trained by the airlines. Once again, Linda was supporting us. That was humiliating.

Then someone told me or I saw an ad about Dade County needing deputies. Since I had experience as an MP in the Marines, Dade County offered to send me to the police academy right away.

I'd never planned on becoming a policeman or a narc. Like other things in life, I just fell into it. I could've ended up being a garbage collector (and, like I said, would've made the same starting salary as I did as a rookie).

But I got lucky, because I loved the narcotics work and was good at it. Of all the jobs I'd ever had, I liked the undercover work best—that, and the smuggling.

For the first few months, I kept to myself in prison. Not socializing with other inmates much was safer for me. The less the other inmates knew about me, the better. Less likely that someone would recognize me or somehow put two and two together and figure out I'd been an undercover agent. I knew what happened to narcs in prison.

Laura wrote me, once in a while, and I talked to her on the phone every weekend. Those calls were rough because she was sad, talking about how I was the love of her life. She was also scared for me in prison, and for her and Julie out there alone. The calls left me lonely—and very horny. One call changed everything.

She'd received a visit from my "boss" a few months after I went to Eglin. Larry, that son of a bitch. He came to the house with a grocery bag full of cash—a "paycheck" for the last job I'd done for him. Larry suggested she work for him, a stewardess being the perfect cover for his line of work, if she was interested in paychecks like he had to offer. I'm sure he wanted a little something more from her too, and how could I compete with his Maserati and his driver and his millions while I was in prison? She didn't take the money, which was good. He wouldn't keep bothering her then. It was craziness, she said, and she didn't want any part of Larry, his business or that whole scene. In fact, she sounded scared shitless.

Larry's visit probably gave her another glimpse into how big our operations were, how much money I'd been making. I didn't ask her if the grocery bag was full, in which case it contained close to $100,000. She told me she refused the cash, which was good, because he wouldn't keep bothering her if she wasn't interested in his money. But that became a turning point in what was left of my relationship with Laura. Well, actually, me going to prison for four years was the big turning point. Larry trying to wow her with cash and the promise of a lucrative career as a stewardess/drug smuggler was just the last straw.

That night, I was so livid about Larry showing up at my house, I couldn't sleep. My stomach burned with indigestion. An hour after lights-out, I was still, fuming, staring at the bunk above me. Laura was only in her late thirties, still a beauty and those stewardesses met pilots and businessmen everywhere. She wouldn't go for someone like Larry, but I knew she wouldn't have any trouble finding a nice respectable man, probably a pilot. Four years was a long time to wait for a drug-smuggling husband, no matter how much she loved me.

Our calls became shorter and a lot less sexy after that phone call. She was always in a hurry to get off the phone.

"Did you get my last letter?" I asked her during one call.

"Yeah ... I just haven't found the time to write. Julie's started kindergarten, you know, so I'm really busy now."

I pressed the phone to my ear and stared at the wall behind the phone. "How's she doing? She like school?"

"She's fine. I haven't told her where you are. She's too young to understand. And I'm not bringing her up—"

"No, don't do that. Prison's no place for kids to be visiting."

"I told her you'd be gone for a while. A long time. For work. But that you"—I could hear her starting to cry—"loved her very much."

I was about to ask Laura to come up for a visit, just her, without Julie, but the thought of her seeing me in prison with nothing to offer her was intolerable. "I miss you two so much. Miss that beautiful face of yours."

The phone line hummed.

Shit! She's shackin' up with somebody else already.

"Rick called last month hoping to talk with you. It was his eighteenth birthday, you know? Sounded hurt that you didn't call him."

I sighed. "What'd you tell him?"

"The truth. I'm not lying for you. He's an adult now, and he deserved to know. I told him where you were. And why you were there. I thought you were going to tell your kids what happened?"

Something welled up inside my chest, anger or the damn helplessness of being locked up. Felt like I'd explode. "Listen, my time's about up here. You and Julie need anything?" Like I could do anything for them from prison.

"No, we're fine. Just take care of yourself in there." The phone was silent for several seconds.

"I'll call you next weekend. Love you, darlin'."

"Yeah, me too."

After that conversation, I started doing some hard time. All my partners got off with no charges and were out there still making money, Laura would find someone else, Julie was fatherless, though maybe not for long, I'd let Lynn and Rick down, Linda was disgusted with me and I'd probably broken my dad's heart—probably literally, with his heart disease.

In prison, everything outside goes on without you, just like if you'd died. The world doesn't stop, or even pause. The world just marches on, and there's not a thing you can do about it. Until you get your mind set that all you have to worry about is what's going on inside those walls and can't change anything going on outside, you'll be miserable. The outside world messes with your head.

My first New Year's Eve in prison, the warden handed out brown paper sacks to all the inmates. Inside were two oranges and an apple. I don't know why, but that took me back to the first New Year's Eve I spent with my first wife. I was a corporal by then, stationed in Hawaii. We were newlyweds, and, man, was I in love with her. She was gorgeous. Might've been pregnant by then, so my first kid on the way. We were at Buzz's Steakhouse, this restaurant with a tiki-hut roof and outdoor dining looking out over

Kailua Beach, eating steak and lobster. The Drifters' song "Up on the Roof" played from the jukebox. I had everything. All I ever wanted, at least at that point in my life. I'd listened to those words about a paradise and felt like *I* was in paradise.

But here I was sitting in prison, peeling oranges and watching *M*A*S*H* reruns.

My first few months in prison, I worked on the grounds crew at the Air Force base, mowing lawns, trimming hedges. I liked watching the airmen moving about the base, occasionally an officer in dress blues or the pilots in their flight suits. Always felt a little regret about not getting my pilot's license. One day, we were clearing litter from the side of a road, and I stepped to the edge of road to allow a truck to pass by. It was late afternoon, and the sun was shining right into my eyes, sort of blinding me for a second, and I stepped too far off the road, right into the roadside ditch. As soon as my foot hit the water, a snake lurched at my ankle and a stabbing pain shot up my leg.

"Ah fuck! Fuck!" I hollered, scrambling from the ditch, hopping over to the road.

A guard ran over, pulled me onto the road, and asked what happened.

I slumped onto the edge of the road. "Snake. In the ditch. Water moccasin, I think. Shit, it's burning all the way up my leg."

He knelt down and pushed my pant leg up, then hollered for another guard to bring a truck over. "Take your boot off before your leg starts swelling."

I took my boot off, then started to feel clammy, cold and

weak. When I tried to lean back on my elbows, the guard said. "No. No. Sit up. Gotta keep your heart above your leg right now." He propped me up until the truck arrived and raced me to the medical building.

By the time we arrived, the bite area and my foot were swollen and gray, like a huge bruise. They gave me a shot, then started me on IV fluids. I was in the clinic for a day or two, having blood tests and getting pain meds. The doctor said I was lucky the bite was low on my leg and hadn't been injected with a large amount of venom. My leg hurt for weeks, but I only got one week off duty, then was given lighter work that I could do with my injury: kitchen duty.

Kitchen duty made for some long days, and it was sweltering in there in the summer. Not as bad as baking in the sun with 90 percent humidity and mosquitoes—and water moccasins—munching on you. I was up at four a.m. to start breakfast for several hundred men, then I got a break before starting lunch. Some days, I worked lunch and dinner shift, starting at ten a.m. to prepare lunch and serving dinner by five-thirty p.m.

The biggest plus to kitchen duty was access to free food. Food was a currency in prison, especially on Friday nights. If an inmate didn't have any visitors, or didn't have anyone to call, he could still soothe his soul with food. In exchange for food, I could get all kinds of commodities: cigarettes, magazines, anything I wanted. Occasionally, I wore a jacket or raincoat over to the kitchen and, before I left, I stuffed the sleeves with desserts or meats, the most sought-after foods. I'd walk by the guards with the coat draped over my arm, careful that my haul wasn't obvious.

Once, only once, I traded food for a line of cocaine. Being high in prison was no good. Cocaine heightened all my senses, but there wasn't anything in prison I wanted to be more aware of. And if I got caught, I went to a higher-security pen. Snorting a line of shitty prison coke wasn't worth the risk. Plus, I wanted out early for good behavior.

CHAPTER 16
THE OTHER SIDE OF MIDNIGHT

Prison time became a little easier after I got assigned to kitchen duty, thanks to that damn water moccasin. I became a businessman, of sorts, with the resources I had access to in the kitchen. That meant I was socializing more with other inmates. Being in prison is just like being on the outside in a lot of ways. Some people are decent, some are bad; some days are good, some bad. A lot more bullshitting goes on inside than on the outside, or maybe the bullshit's just more concentrated, and you can't easily get away from it. I didn't pay any attention to rumors or what inmates said about each other. What a man *said* didn't matter much to me, what he *did* was what really mattered. So, I watched what people did, just like when I was on the force.

Most of the men who I talked with I considered business associates; we exchanged goods and helped each other get whatever we needed to make our time more comfortable. A friend in prison is rare. That's true on the outside too, or at least it had been in my lines of work. A few men at Eglin I eventually considered friends. Gustavo was one of them.

Gustavo had a Spanish accent, but his English was flawless, obviously well-schooled. At Eglin, he worked in the laundry room, though I'm sure he never did his own, let alone anyone else's, laundry on the outside. We were all allowed to wear our own clothes when we were off-duty, and Gustavo wore slacks and nice button-down shirts. If he'd had on a tie, he could've passed for a businessman. I'm pretty sure that's what he was—a cocaine businessman—because his brothers flew in from Colombia on a Learjet every couple of months to visit. They weren't doing that just to bring Gustavo cookies and new underwear. No, I'm sure he was still helping his brothers run the family business.

Other prisoners talked about Gustavo, probably because he was obviously a powerful, wealthy Colombian man. But I ignored the rumors about him using his money to control other inmates. I just took my time and got to know him. Clearly, he had enough money to pay another inmate to do just about anything for him. But I don't think Gustavo just wanted to avoid menial tasks like making his bed every morning. I think his cubicle-mate needed money, so Gustavo paid him to make his bed and straighten their cubicle every day. He was paying his roommate out of generosity and doing it in a way that preserved his roommate's dignity. I respected that.

Gustavo frequently bought or traded for food with me or the guys who worked in the commissary. I learned quickly what he liked, usually the desserts, and snuck his favorites out or set one aside so he'd have one when he came through the line.

Eventually, Gustavo and I started playing racquetball a few times a week and were well-matched, giving each other a good workout. I nurtured a relationship with him, talking to him every day, and not just about our prior business as smugglers. We talked about life, even about partnering later outside. We never made any plans, just talked about how we'd enjoy working together. We always left the idea open.

Near the end of my third year in prison, as I was getting ready to petition the parole board for early release, Laura served me with divorce papers. I can't honestly say I was surprised. The terms were that she retained full custody of Julie and she requested no child support. As I read those words, I dropped down onto my bed with a thud. No child support. That meant she didn't want me visiting Julie; she was cutting me completely out of their lives. She found someone else. So much for waiting for me. What could I do, sitting there inside and looking at two years of parole when I *did* get out? I pounded my fist into the mattress. I didn't have much of a case to fight for any kind of custody from prison. And what sense was there in fighting to pay child support when I was sure that I now had no money left.

Before I went to Eglin, I'd banked over $100,000 to support Laura and Julie, and hoped there'd be some money left when I got out. I also had twelve high-quality, uncut emeralds in a safe-deposit box. Each emerald was about as big as my thumbnail. Those gems were worth a nice little chunk of change, the change I planned to use to get back on my feet after my release. If Laura was willing to forego any child support, that meant she had plenty of money, and that meant she'd cleaned me out. I was sure the bank account was now empty. Probably the safe-deposit box was also empty.

I talked to my attorney, who confirmed what I suspected —I was in no position to fight any of this: divorce terms, custody, even the status of a bank account and safe-deposit box in Laura's name. Not from federal prison.

After I signed the paperwork and the divorce was final, I received a box from Laura. It contained photos of Julie and me, clothes and a new pair of Sperry Top-Siders, the kind that didn't aggravate my old foot injury. How thoughtful of the cheating bitch.

Going through a second divorce got me thinking a lot about what I'd put Linda and the kids through, what I'd had, what I'd thrown away. From my current vantage point, my early life with her looked pretty idyllic. We used to put the kids to bed then go out to the pool and skinny-dip. That patio was fenced off from the neighbor's view, and we'd keep all the lights off. We'd get a little wild there on the pool steps. We had a lot fun nights out there.

I even got up the nerve to write Linda a letter from prison. Told her I was sorry for walking out on her, that leaving her was one of the worst decisions of my life and marrying her had been one of the best. If she could ever see a future where we could be together again, I wrote, I'd jump at the chance.

She wrote back basically saying, *No thanks.*

After three and a half years of incarceration, I was approved for early release due to good behavior. As they processed the paperwork for my release, the parole board found one issue. Before I could be released, I had to pay all the back child support that I owed Linda. Several thousand dollars. At the time, I was mad. All my money gone, taken by two ex-wives. But when I went to Lynn's high-school graduation a month later, Linda told me she planned to use that back child support to pay for Lynn's college tuition. After all the support I failed to provide over the years, I was actually sending one of my kids to college. In retrospect, probably one of the best uses of my drug money.

I arranged for my attorney to complete all the paperwork and pay the child support, and I was released. A free man. Here's what freedom looked like for me: Laura had sold the house and left no forwarding address. My bank account was still open with about $8,000 in it. After I paid the back child support, I had $19.75 left. I left prison with no car, no house and nineteen bucks.

My parole officer made arrangements for me to live in a halfway house just outside of downtown Miami. The building was in a lower-class neighborhood with large, dilapidated houses. This one was divided into several bedrooms, a small living room, a dining room and one big kitchen with two refrigerators and two stoves. The ceilings were yellowed from cigarette smoke, and the house always reeked of fried food. But the manager required that we keep the house and the yard tidy. Dinner was provided at six p.m. in a dining room with three rickety tables. Residents could use the kitchen to make their own breakfast and lunch but had to provide their own food for those meals.

My bedroom had a saggy twin bed, an even saggier couch, a small TV and a shared bathroom between my room and the adjacent one. Eight other parolees lived there, but everyone usually kept to themselves. Sometimes a few of us watched TV in the living room, or played a game of poker to fill the empty evenings.

For the past three and a half years, I was mostly free to move about the prison and grounds, but my time was highly structured. And someone had always been accounting for my whereabouts. For the first week in that halfway house, I always felt like I needed to be somewhere, to be—counted. It took me some time to get used to that kind of freedom. I drifted through the days, skimmed the Help Wanted ads and chatted with the other men in the house, but many evenings I found myself wishing I was back in Eglin. There, I'd at least been surrounded by people, even a couple of friends, had a job, a reputation, a goal of getting out. That halfway house and that time was miserable for me.

I was required to report once a month to my parole officer. Everything about my P.O., James, looked and sounded exhausted: his posture, his face, his monotone speech. He was about my age, mid-forties, overweight, chain-smoked and his raspy voice led me to believe he'd done so for many years. I wasn't allowed to leave the county without his permission, and he made it clear that he could check on me any time, day or night, anywhere, and request a urine test without notice. My first goal, James said, was to get a job.

I'd already put in a couple of applications. Felony convictions are not that great on a resume. The next application I put in, I made up a job for the past few years.

Forget about cook at Eglin, I was listing real estate agent. Getting a real estate job now wasn't an option, because the housing market crashed while I was in prison. Maybe cars again; I was good at sales. What I really wanted to do was start my own business. Self-employment suited me, especially now with a criminal history. I just didn't have the seed money, thanks to Laura.

Whenever I thought about Laura, my money or those emeralds, I felt like exploding. At night, in bed, I fantasized about saving up enough money to pay a hitman to hunt Laura down and cut her thumbs off. Teach her a lesson about stealing my money. Even thought about who I'd hire. Luckily, for me and her, by the time I had enough money for a hitman, I had more important things on my mind.

CHAPTER 17
BACK IN BUSINESS

A few weeks after getting paroled, Gustavo called the halfway house looking for me. He was still in prison and asked if I'd come visit him. He wanted to introduce me to his brothers who would be visiting that Saturday afternoon—from Colombia.

Friday afternoon, I asked another man at the halfway house if I could borrow his truck for the weekend, said I had a job tearing down an old barn for a friend. James wouldn't let me go visit a prisoner, so I didn't bother asking for permission. If he called or came looking for me, story would be the same: friend paid me to tear down a barn then offered to put me up and feed me for the night. Just hoped, if it came to that, he wouldn't ask for the friend's name and number.

My hands were sweating as I drove out of the county before dawn Saturday morning. Drove the exact speed limit the entire nine-hour drive.

When I walked into the lobby of the motel near the

prison compound where I was to meet Gustavo—he had those privileges for off-site visits—he was there with two other men. He introduced me to his brothers. Rafael looked similar to Gustavo and had straight, short hair brushed back over his head, a little gray at his temples. Nicolás, they called him Nico, was much younger, with a darker complexion and longer, wavy brown hair. I spoke as much Spanish as I could to Rafael and Nico, which wasn't necessary as they both spoke fluent English.

We went into one of the motel rooms and they began searching every surface, running their hands over the door jambs, mattresses, bedframes, chairs, night stands, ashtrays. I checked the lamp bases, the mouth- and earpieces of the phone then unscrewed the ceiling light fixture and popped off the ends of the curtain rods. I even made sure there weren't any hangers with cardboard tubes. No bugs anywhere.

Nico and Rafael sat on the foot of the bed, and Gustavo and I pulled two chairs over and huddled up. Gustavo started the conversation. "John, I asked you here to talk business. During our time together"—he pointed in the direction of the prison—"I came to know you and trust you a great deal. You're a good man—for a gringo." We all chuckled, and I appreciated the break in the tension. He gestured at his brothers. "I've talked with my family about you, and we would like to do business with you."

Being asked into this circle of men, even though his brothers watched me closely, *was* a huge sign of trust. And respect. They were trying to get a read on me, and that was fine, because I was doing the same. If this was going to work and develop into a fruitful business relationship, we all had to trust each other.

"Well, I'm honored. I have a great deal of respect for you, and I'd love to do business with your family. What'd you have in mind?"

"Our next shipment is arriving in Miami next month," Rafael said, putting his thumb to his nose to mimic snorting blow. My pulse quickened. I'd hoped that was why he invited me up. This could be my way out of that sorry-ass halfway house.

"Cuanto?" I asked.

Nico looked at Rafael then Gustavo, who nodded.

"One hundred," Nico said.

Now my heart was really racing. I pursed my lips and nodded, scanning my memory for contacts I could rekindle, but it'd been almost four years. And I'd never moved that much cocaine. A hundred kilos of marijuana, definitely, and way more. But never that much cocaine. A hundred kilos was a lot of blow.

"I have to be honest with you here. I'd love to have access to some of your product, not all of it … maybe a quarter of it but … it'd have to be on the arm. Due to my recent vacation"—now *I* thumbed in the direction of the prison—"I just don't have that kind of cash right now." I shook my head slightly, mostly in frustration, because I really wanted to work with them.

No one said anything for a few seconds, painful seconds for me as I wondered if I'd blown the deal. Gustavo was still looking at me and stroking his chin pensively. Then he looked over at his brothers and spoke to them in Spanish, gesturing with his hands as he talked. I stepped over to the table where there was an ashtray and lit a cigarette. I couldn't pick up enough of Gustavo's words to make out what he was saying but hoped he was convincing them to front me some product. They both nodded while he spoke. Then Rafael asked Nico something. He replied.

Finally, Gustavo walked over to the table. I crushed my cigarette out in the ashtray.

"This is fine. On the arm. Viente. You pay us after you sell it." Gustavo extended his hand, and as I shook it, he slapped my shoulder. Rafael and Nico joined us around the table and we all shook on it.

"I'm looking forward to a successful business relationship with your family," I said. Then I added with a smile, "And, Gustavo, if I ever come to you and ask for a hundred kilos, you better believe I'm settin' you up." Everybody released another of those tension-lowering laughs.

Forming a new business arrangement was always tense because you don't know who you can trust, but you've got to lay all your cards on the table, so to speak, or no deals can be made. When you get to that point of openness in a business arrangement, the tension drops, everybody starts to relax, no one's dancing around trying to hide anything or impress anyone or get a bigger share of the money or drugs. Everybody can finally be themselves.

I always used humor and laughter as a good indicator, both undercover and smuggling, of when a group reaches this stage. When I saw people relax, I knew I was "in" with a dealer or smuggling group. Suppose I used laughter to get "in" too, to break the ice and put people at ease.

Before we left the motel room, Gustavo handed me a piece of paper with a number written on it and directed me to call that number when I was ready to pick up the product.

"If I'm not there," Nico said, "just ask for Javi. He can set you up too."

I was "in" like I'd never been before. All I needed to do was call a number and get twenty kilos of what I imagined was high-quality cocaine. Twenty kilos.

Driving back to Miami, I was on top of the world. Gustavo wasn't bullshitting me. His family flew into the country to meet *me*. Sitting there with a Colombian family of that caliber solidified that I was legit. I didn't have to con anyone to be there or to do business with them. They believed what I could and couldn't do. Man, some Colombians shot people for being dishonest, but I wasn't worried about that. I would never lie to this family and would always make good on every deal.

Unfortunately, a month just wasn't enough time for me to put a deal together. I'd lost too many contacts. Four years is a long time in the smuggling business; there's lots of turnover and people tend to disappear. I'd heard Larry was still rolling in the business, but I wasn't working with him again. After everyone in my old group had gotten off scot-free, I felt like I'd taken a fall for those guys. I'm not saying someone snitched, though I'd never know for sure, but I did a full sentence by keeping my mouth shut. And then while I was sitting in prison, Larry was hitting on my wife —now ex-wife. I wasn't about to stir up my anger about all of that, so I steered clear of my old partners.

I hated to let Gustavo's family down, not on the first run. Here I had this great connection, access to lots of stuff but didn't know anyone I could rely on who could move that much for me. As much as I hated to do it, I finally called the number that Gustavo had given me. I told Javi how sorry I was but couldn't take any of the coke this month, maybe next month. I was humiliated. No problem, he told me. Just call next month when I was ready.

What an awful day that was for me. Nothing was coming together for me on the outside. With a felony on my record, I couldn't find a decent job, had no money, was living in a shitty halfway house and couldn't put together an op to move twenty kilos of what I suspected was probably pure Colombian cocaine. For the first time in my life, I was afraid I wasn't going to make it. Maybe I'd be one of those guys who lived in a halfway house for a year, riding the bus to a job at McDonald's until I could afford an old junker of a car.

A few weeks later, this old man, maybe mid-sixties, who I'd met in prison called me. He lived up in Georgia. He'd been released from prison right before me and said he might look me up on the outside, but I never expected to hear from him. Drug trafficking wasn't his thing. His arrest had been for food-stamp fraud. But, just like me, he was looking for work. When I described what I had access to, he told me about some bad boys up in Atlanta, who he was sure would buy all the cocaine we had available. As I listened to him talk, I realized he was the perfect partner: he had connections, his connections were nowhere near Miami (or more importantly, near me), he wasn't interested in snorting blow himself and he looked like an old farmer with overalls, paunch belly, scruffy whiskers and gray hair sticking up all over. Not a suspicious-looking character.

Next, I contacted Roger, a smuggler I knew from before

my vacation. He was a big, burly man—well-fed, I soon learned—who also worked for Larry in the past. Our paths had crossed several months before I was arrested when we were both meeting up to get paid. After Larry handed us our grocery sacks, I looked at Roger's bag and said, "Man, I gotta work with you. Your grocery bag's a whole lot bigger than mine." We both laughed and agreed that we should talk. We ran into each other a few more times after that and got to know each other; smugglers in Miami hung out at a lot of the same nightclubs and hotels. He was a good guy and we'd started talking about putting a deal together, but then I got popped.

Roger seemed glad to hear from me and to hear that I was back in the game. He wanted to meet right away. Said he and his partner, Jack, were looking to put some kind of deal together.

Next thing you know, I'm discussing business with Roger and Jack, who turns out is his son. A grown son, like in his mid-twenties. After an hour or so, we reached agreement on several points. Then Roger said, "Man, one last thing. You can't do this from no halfway house. It's crazy enough doing this on parole, but that's your business. But smuggling from a halfway house'll bring too much heat. Just come and stay at my place until you get on your feet."

How pathetic and needy did he think I was? "Nah, couldn't do that."

"Ah, do it," Jack said. "You can stay in my old room. Mom'll love having someone else to cook for."

"And I won't make you call me Pops," Roger said, laughing. "Seriously. My wife won't mind at all."

I held my hand up in front of me. "I appreciate the offer, but I don't want any handouts."

He stared at me for several seconds. "It's not a handout, it's a business decision. Think of it as better cover for you than a fuckin' halfway house for ex-cons. Besides, if this Colombian family's coke is as good as you think, after the first run you'll have your own apartment, car and anything else you want."

I nodded. "True." And I did want out of that halfway house. He made some good points. But the principle of it … I didn't take handouts. Never had and never would.

"Just come for dinner. Maureen wants to meet you."

"Alright, alright, Pops," I said, and we all laughed.

"Hell, you're older than me. I should call *you* Pops," Roger said.

That name stuck. Throughout the rest of our partnership, Roger always called me Pops.

Maureen cooked a heavenly meal that first night: tender, juicy medium-rare steaks crusted with herbs and garlic mashed potatoes. My wall of refusal was crumbling.

Then Roger and Jack started talking business, drug business, right in front of Maureen over dinner. My jaw about dropped open. She was clearly in the know, and I made a mental note to ask Roger how he managed that. I figured she accepted his business for one of two reasons: she either loved the cocaine or she loved the money. From the hole that eventually formed in her septum, I figured it was the cocaine.

After dinner, she whipped up dessert: bananas, a scoop of vanilla ice cream, rum poured over it all then set aflame. Any resistance to moving in with them melted away.

What a relief it was to live in a home where the smuggling was fully out in the open. Their house wasn't over-the-top like some smuggler's had, but it was spacious and well-kept. A luxury after a few years in prison and a couple months in that cruddy old halfway house.

The attorney who represented me during my trial set up a business for me. I called it Pro Polishing, a company in which I, supposedly, traveled around to detail and polish cars at people's homes or businesses. I needed this company to launder the money I planned to bring in from my smuggling; not all of the money, because I planned to bring in way more than I could justify from a car-polishing company. But a "legitimate" business would help. The rest of the money I'd spend, hide, invest and, hopefully, use to wine and dine some fine ladies. This business would also be critical for explaining my revenue stream to my P.O. when my money began to roll in.

As we began to plan our operation, we all agreed to start small, an amount we could easily sell in one month, so we could establish a successful, strong relationship with Gustavo's family. For our first run, we decided to ask for just ten kilos. I called Nico and Javi in Miami, and we were off and running.

Roger reserved two rental cars in a fake name. One car Jack would use to deliver cocaine to a couple of his contacts around Miami, and Roger and I used the second car to deliver Farmer John his portion at a rendezvous hotel near the Georgia-Florida border.

The day after my monthly parole check-in with James, we completed our first deal. After we paid the $160,000 we owed for fronting us ten kilos, there was over $300,000 profit to split up between me, Roger, Jack and Farmer John. I gave Roger 10 percent of my proceeds as payment for feeding me and putting me up at his house. For the first time in years, I was taking care of business and supporting myself, not depending on the prison system or a handout from a friend.

It felt good to be back.

CHAPTER 18
A PERFECT DAY

After that first deal, I bought a pickup truck, a used one so my P.O. wouldn't get suspicious, but it was in mint condition. I rented a furnished apartment, went shopping for some nice slacks and buttoned shirts. When I pulled up at James' office in a new truck, but purposely wearing old jeans and a t-shirt, he whistled and said, "Nice truck. Your new business must be doing well."

"Yep. Needed a decent vehicle to get to customers and carry all my supplies. It's used, so I got a good deal. I put some flyers up, got some customers from word-of-mouth. I'm gettin' calls from all over Miami to polish cars."

"This a legit business or what? You have to be working or looking for work."

"It's legit. Had my attorney file the corporation paperwork and everything. He said I'd get better tax breaks if I incorporated."

"Got a number?"

"Of my attorney? Sure." I scribbled his number down on

a piece of paper. "I'm happy to bring the corporation filing for you to look at."

He took the number and said, "Yeah. Why don't you bring that next time."

"Sure thing. I'll even give your car a polish and detail if you want. Just say the word. Friend-of-the-family deal. Thirty-five bucks for the full package." I grinned at him. No response. He never smiled, laughed, nothing.

The other thing I did as soon as I got my first "paycheck" was ask a woman out on a date. Maureen had been trying to introduce me to her friend, Suzy, but I'd refused. How romantic to invite a lady over to Roger and Maureen's house for dinner and then into their spare bedroom where I was bunking. Smooth, real smooth. I would've loved a date but couldn't see that happening until I had a car, an apartment and some money. What was I going to do, have Roger drive us to a restaurant?

After we made that first deal and I had some cash, Maureen invited Suzy over for dinner. She had strawberry-blond hair and a few freckles, not really my type, but was cute, tall and had a nice body. Most importantly, she was fun, laughing easily at all my jokes, and I told her the truth about my past. Not about my present, though, not yet. My prison time didn't seem to faze her, and we had a great time that first night. When she left, we made plans to go out to dinner the next weekend. I told her to wear something fancy.

I picked her up at her apartment the next weekend and she looked fine in a snug black dress, heels and smelled fine, too, like some expensive perfume but worn lightly, just a hint when I stood near her. We went to a restaurant

Maureen suggested. When I made the reservation, I asked for their most private table. That meal was perfect: fresh lobster and champagne in a secluded booth in the back of the restaurant. Man, was I happy: cash to spend, a nice-looking fun woman, good food.

After we ate, I slid into her side of the booth, scooching close. "I've got a bottle of Dom Perignon on ice back at my place." I pushed her hair back and kissed her neck, breathing in her perfume. "Mmm, you smell good."

She turned towards me, and I kissed her. I was moving pretty fast, but a few years in prison will do that. She didn't seem to mind.

"Let's go get some of that champagne," she murmured.

I jumped up, dropped two hundred dollars on the table and reached for her hand.

"Don't you want your change?" She looked at the hundreds on the table.

"No time for that. I got more important things to do." I mock-dragged her to my truck and was encouraged by the sound of her laughter behind me. And the click of her heels.

Those heels were the first thing to come off as we sipped champagne and rolled around on the couch. By the time half the bottle was gone, her earrings were on the coffee table, and I was working on the zipper of her tight little dress.

"Now I haven't been with a lady since I got out of the pen," I mumbled. "But I think everything still works."

She rubbed up against me and smiled. "Feels like every-thing's still workin' down there."

"We better go upstairs and check."

The next morning, as I headed out of my bedroom, Suzy

asked me to make her some coffee. "Sure thing," I said. "I'll even make you a killer Denver omelet. Come on down when you're ready."

Down in the kitchen, I formed a couple of lines of coke on the table. Suzy seemed like the type that might like some nose candy, and I didn't want to be sneaking around hiding who I really was all the time. I was sick of doing that. Figured the sooner we got this out in the open, the better.

She shuffled into the kitchen wearing one of my t-shirts, just as I was about to snort one of those lines through a rolled-up dollar bill. She paused, took in the scene then looked at me. I offered the dollar-bill straw to her.

She took the straw and smiled. "Guess I won't be needing that coffee then."

I knew then my life was taking a turn for the better.

This time around, things were going to be different. I planned to keep the smuggling manageable. With my connection to Gustavo and their willingness to front me the drugs, I didn't need a moneyman. This Colombia family trusted me with their product and that was worth more than any amount of money. I could run my own show, no one else calling the shots. Now *I* chose who I worked with and who I didn't, how many kilos we brought in and who we sold it to.

My relationship with the Colombians went deeper than that. More than just the value of the fronted product, once I proved myself—that I could deliver the money back to them—I could ask them for any amount of cocaine. The more I asked for, the better the price and the higher our profit. My relationship with Gustavo meant unlimited access.

Roger, Jack, Farmer John and I were a good team, worked well together. We increased our runs to twenty kilos, but no more than that. We didn't want to introduce more unknowns, more risks, like bringing in new distributors or selling to different dealers. Manageable is what we wanted.

A week before Thanksgiving, Farmer John called for some coke, so I called to confirm that my connection could supply what we needed in a couple of days, Roger reserved the rental car, we picked up the coke and drove it up to Macon, Georgia. Bringin' home the bacon from Macon, we called it. Usually, when we delivered kilos to Farmer John, he came back the next evening with the money stuffed in grain sacks and old tool boxes in the back of his beat-up 1960 Bronco. He was that good.

But during this trip, he didn't come back the next morning, calling to say he needed another day. It's the holiday, he explained, it's hard to reach folks. But the second morning, no Farmer John. No word from him. No money.

We really started worrying then. Dealers don't exactly take holidays off. In fact, they're usually busier during the holidays. Our worst fears were that something happened to him—and to our coke. Maybe he'd been arrested or someone stole the coke. It never entered my mind that he would rat us out. But if he didn't return with the money, then we owed the Colombians a few hundred thousand dollars. Now, we had lots of cash stashed away, but pulling that much together would've been difficult, would've cleaned me out for sure. But we couldn't go back to Nico or Javi without the money. If I did that, it could put a big dent in our ops, not to mention my reputation with the Colombians.

We couldn't do anything but sit tight. Sit tight, wait and worry. We didn't know anything about Farmer John's connections, only that most of them were in Atlanta, some in South Carolina, maybe Tennessee. But we had no idea where he'd gone with this load. Roger called Maureen and told her to postpone Thanksgiving dinner until we returned.

The hotel we stayed at this time was the Best Western just outside of Macon. It had a sweeping, curved staircase up one side of the lobby, leading to an open landing above the front desk. When we had to leave our room so we didn't go stir-crazy, we lounged around on that second-story landing. From there, we could see the front door, but the front-desk staff couldn't see us above them.

There wasn't much happening in Macon the day before Thanksgiving. It wasn't exactly a hopping city to begin with. So, we started dipping into our cocaine stash a little more than usual. James was on vacation, so I wasn't worried about getting drug-tested when I got back. By the end of the second day, we were hitting our stash pretty hard. We holed up in that hotel, worried shitless, wired out of our minds on blow and tried not to draw any unwanted attention from the staff.

Late on the third morning, Farmer John showed up with all of our money, like it was no big deal. Turned out his connection in Atlanta was out of town that first day, but then when he got back, was all suspicious he'd been followed and was being watched by the police. So he asked Farmer John just sit on the product for a couple days, which he did. Farmer John finally told the guy that if he wanted this shit, now was the time. They found a new meeting location and made the exchange.

That whole scene sounded too hot for my liking. For all we knew, Farmer John's contact had worn a wire when they made the exchange. We packed our suitcases of cash into the trunk and hit the road. Made it back to Miami in eight hours, record time, watching our rearview mirror the whole way.

When we got home, Maureen and Suzy had a Thanksgiving feast spread out on the table.

After dinner, Maureen opened up a bottle of wine from their collection—a 1961 Chateau Latour. She uncorked it and told us to leave it alone for a while so the wine could breathe.

"What? I ain't got time to wait for a bottle of wine to breathe," I said. "I need a drink, woman. Now! A real drink. Roger, where's your scotch?"

Suzy rolled her eyes. "Just ignore him. He can wait." I pulled her down next to me on the sofa, and she swatted at me.

"Believe me, this wine will be worth the wait. Right, sweetie?" Maureen said, nestling into the couch next to Roger.

Roger put his arm around her shoulders and rubbed her arm, up and down, smiling. "Oh, it's worth the wait, all right."

We each snorted a line of cocaine while Roger and I described our nerve-racking journey of the past few days. Then Maureen poured us each a glass of this wine, told us to swirl it around a bit. I could not believe how good that wine tasted. To me, wine was always musty and made my mouth pucker, but this was rich and smooth, almost woodsy. That was the only wine I ever enjoyed.

We had suitcases full of money, a tray of cocaine on the table, full stomachs and this bottle of wine. The four of us sat there for hours talking and dreaming, and I didn't need to pretend to be someone else, or think about what I was saying to who or check the back rooms, under lamps or out the windows. And for once, I didn't snort more than a couple of lines. After all the coke and anxiety of the past few days, sweating it out in that hotel, my body was spent. Thanksgiving dinner, the wine and just a little cocaine mellowed me out. I hadn't felt that content in years. Everything was perfect.

CHAPTER 19
ADULTS

When I went up to Ohio for Lynn's high-school graduation, Rick asked about my arrest and time at Eglin. Rick told me he and his girlfriend, Vanessa, were dealing marijuana to make extra money. He'd dropped out of high school and wasn't making much money working as a cook. The way they were smoking weed every day, I'm sure their dealing helped support their habit too.

I didn't think about him being my son or about him getting further into dealing or about him ever getting caught. And I never imagined he'd get strung out. Like he was any other small-town dealer who I wanted to introduce to some world-class cocaine, I asked him if he ever moved any cocaine.

"Nah," Rick said, "we don't come across cocaine much up here. Even if I did, wouldn't be able to afford it. That blow's too rich for my blood."

"Well, let's see what kind of coke you can get up here. I'll pay for it, and we'll check it out."

He looked over at Vanessa then back to me. "You wanna buy some coke? For us to check out?" He motioned with his index finger back and forth between us. "Together. To … snort together?"

I nodded.

"How much?"

I shrugged. "Whatever you can get. Few hundred bucks' worth."

He made some calls and came back the next evening with an eighth of an ounce of cocaine. Tossing it on the table, he said, "Got an eight-ball. I gotta say, this is weird as shit, using with my old man. But, what the hell. Let's do some blow."

"Let's see what we got here first. Vanessa, you got some bleach? Need about half a glass, a small one."

She returned with a jar and slid it across the table to me.

"Watch what happens. The impurities will drop out first, and the coke will float on the top for a while then slowly glide to the bottom." I sprinkled a pinch of coke over the bleach. We all watched the powder drop straight to the bottom of the glass. A smattering of coke floated. "This ain't coke. It's full of cut."

"This don't have any coke in it? I just paid four hundred bucks for this cocaine. *Your* four hundred."

"Oh, it has some cocaine, but not much. I wouldn't snort this shit." I scooted the baggie across the table to them.

"You ain't gonna snort any?" he said.

I shook my head.

"We'll snort it, if that's okay with you. It was your money," Vanessa asked.

"Well, I ain't goin' back for a refund," Rick said.

"Go on. Snort away," I said.

Vanessa rolled up a dollar bill. "Cool. We can never afford this shit."

Rick tapped some out on the table, made two lines and snorted it. Sniffing hard, he said, "Whew! That burns like a motha fucker."

"That's another thing," I told them. "Good coke doesn't burn like that. If you ever wanna get your hands on some good stuff, lemme know. I'll set you up. If this is the best stuff around, you could make a lotta money up here with my stuff."

They glanced at each other and smiled.

After that visit, Rick was real interested in seeing me, and I was pretty sure it wasn't to rekindle a relationship with his long-lost dad. Looking back, that probably *was* part of his trips down to Miami, to get to know me again. But I couldn't see that or didn't want to. Me and Rick were so far gone into drug use. Not exactly a solid foundation for a father-son relationship.

He and Vanessa, along with her daughter—who was maybe four or five—drove down to Miami for his twenty-first birthday. He asked about this amazing blow I'd told him about. Rick sure didn't beat around the bush; he never had. The first time we snorted together, just a couple of lines, was that weekend. I told myself we were just celebrating his birthday, my style.

I stayed at Roger's house so they could stay in my apartment. In the closet of my apartment, was a fresh kilo of cocaine stashed in a cooler. I wasn't hauling it over to Roger's, but thought they should be aware, with a little kid there and all, that a kilo was stashed in the closet.

I showed them the bedroom, which had a brand new, king-size waterbed. "Now, when you kids get tired of playing on that waterbed, you might wanna try some of this." I motioned for them to follow me to the hall closet. I lifted the lid to one of the coolers and cut a tiny slit in the plastic wrapped around the kilo and broke off a chunk of cocaine. It was the pure stuff, right off the plane from South America. Uncut. Man, that stuff was beautiful, full of dense, golden-colored, crystalline flakes.

Their eyes were about bugging out of the heads.

"Now, I'm telling you, go easy on this stuff. It's uncut. Understand?"

They both nodded but I could tell from the craving in their faces they weren't listening.

"I'm serious."

"Let's give it a try," Rick said. "Let's start celebratin' my birthday."

We went to the kitchen and Rick chopped some up with his driver's license, made this long line and started rolling up a dollar bill. I assumed he'd share that line with me and Vanessa, but before I could say anything, he leaned over the counter and snuffed that entire line up his nose.

"I don't think you heard me, son. This is *pure* coke." I pointed at the pile remaining on the counter. "As pure as it gets. Like ninety seven percent cocaine. Right outta the South American jungle. You have to build up to a line like that. Unless you've been snorting the good stuff for—"

"I'm fine." Rick waved his hand at me, dismissing my concern.

I raised my eyebrows and watched him for a long moment, then shrugged. "If you say so."

Vanessa started to chop up another line when the blow finally kicked in for Rick. His face was flushed, his pupils huge. He was lit up. "Whoa. You ain't kiddin', man. Nessa, wait 'til you try it. This is some *good* shit."

"Why don't you make this line a little smaller, Vanessa. Just for starters," I said.

She nodded and started forming a more reasonable line. Rick's face was getting a little pale and sweaty. Before she snorted the line, she looked over at him. "Y'alright, Rick?"

"Uh … I don't know. I don't feel so hot." He glanced at me then bolted to the bathroom.

Vanessa and I stared at each other while we listened to him heaving in the toilet.

"Like I said, you gotta build up tolerance for this pure stuff. He'll be fine."

She tapped her driver's license next to the line she'd made, which was half the size of the one Rick just snorted. "How 'bout we split this one?"

"That's my girl."

When we were high, Rick just seemed like my—I don't know, not really friends because he was so much younger than me—using buddy. Drugs make "friends" out of people from all walks of life. In a way, that was preferable, because I was consumed with smuggling and using cocaine, while hiding everything from my parole officer, so didn't have time or energy to keep up a façade with people who I saw regularly. And I started seeing Rick real regular. I think we both knew what was going on there. But he was an adult by then. He didn't need a father anymore. It was too late for all that.

Now, when Lynn started popping into my life again,

that was different. She was barely eighteen, and guess I still felt protective of her. The first time she came down to Miami with a college roommate, I could tell she was using cocaine and figured she got it from Rick, least I hoped she had. At least, that way, I knew she was snorting good quality, not some junk all cut with God knows what. And getting it from him was safer than from some idiot on the streets.

I didn't tell Lynn I was smuggling cocaine like I had with Rick. She was in college and, even if she partied occasionally, I wasn't about to start giving her a bunch of coke. So I just waited to see how our new relationship unfolded and left the ball in her court in terms of talking about drugs, cocaine and my line of work.

Things were different with Rick. And the day he started dealing for me wasn't one of my better days. If I hadn't been so deep into smuggling and snorting by then, that day might've been a warning sign. It should've been. But the only warning signs I paid attention to, by then, were those related to getting busted again or getting ripped off. On the day Rick started working for me, any boundary I previously held between right and wrong, good and bad, was long gone. Honest to God, I wasn't even aware I was crossing that boundary, or that I'd let go of that boundary years earlier. In my mind, I still had some principles that I lived by.

CHAPTER 20
BAD BUSINESS

Within a couple of weeks of Rick's visit to Miami, he called to say some guy he knew had pieced together $4,000 to buy some coke from me. Rick was willing to come down to Florida to pick it up, but this guy, Mike, wanted to come along. He wouldn't hand over his money until he had the merchandise in hand. I didn't want to interact with some small-time punk from Ohio who I didn't know; could've been a setup for all I knew. Didn't sound like Rick knew him too well either. And all for a few ounces of blow? Wasn't worth the risk. And I wasn't about to start fronting stuff to a stranger, even though Rick assured me Mike had the money and was reliable. I didn't like the situation.

The whole deal started to be way more trouble than four ounces was worth, to me anyways. I understood that four ounces was a big deal for Mike. Mainly, I was working this deal out as a favor to Rick. I'm sure he was getting some of the product or profit or both, since Rick was the one with the connection to Miami, to me.

After we dickered over the phone for a couple of days, I finally said to Rick, "Listen. I'll just fly up and make a delivery. You can introduce me and Mike. We'll make the exchange. Bada-bing. I go back home. Then you guys do your thing."

"How you gonna get the shit through the airport?"

"Ah, don't worry about that. Done it before. I got my ways. I'm the *man!*"

The phone was silent for a few seconds.

"Alright. If you want to. When?"

"Few days. I'll call you when I have my ticket."

A few days later, I duct-taped four ounces in a few little baggies to my waist, got dressed, walked through Miami International security and flew up to Columbus.

When I got to Rick's house he was there with Vanessa, Mike and a guy named Mark. They were all sitting in the living room, drinking beers and smoking cigs. Rick introduced me around. Everyone seemed nervous. The tension in the room wasn't the usual tension of new people doing business. It was more intense than that. I took in what was going on: lot of fidgeting, nail-biting, no one talking, little eye contact.

Maybe Rick told them I was his dad. That *would* be weird for a bunch of twenty-something small-time dealers. Or maybe he'd told them I'd just been released from prison and was on parole, worried I might bring some heat to them. Whatever it was, I didn't like the feel of that room and was contemplating my next move. I didn't know who the hell this Mark guy was. He wouldn't make eye contact with me or anyone else in the room, just stared at the TV, which was muted, and sucked hard on a cigarette, one draw after another, with hardly a breath between them. His eyes were dark, huge pupils—either already wasted or very nervous. Mark was sitting at the end of the couch. Then I noticed a sawed-off shotgun right next to him, propped between the couch and the wall.

"Hey Rick, how about a drink? I been on that plane for hours. Got anything besides beer?" I jerked my head towards the kitchen.

In the kitchen, I said quietly, "What's goin' on out there? And who's the guy with the damn shotgun?"

"Who, Mark? That's Lynn's ex-boyfriend. Think he's gonna sell some of it, he put in a little money. He takes that gun everywhere. Brought it in case somethin' goes haywire. He's alright, just a little paranoid."

I was glad to hear this shotgun-carrying fool was now her ex. "You need to get him, and that gun, outta here. You hear me? I'm not doing a deal with some nut sittin' around with a sawed-off shotgun. Mike's got all the money?"

"Yeah, he's got it."

"Then nothin's gonna go wrong here. The shotgun's gotta go, though."

Rick stared at me for a few seconds, then nodded.

I went into the bathroom to peel off the bags of coke. As I was pulling the tape off, I could hear Rick talking, then someone else mumbling. I assumed it was Mark. I paused to listen, waiting to hear if Mark was escalating things. Then I heard the front door open and close.

When I walked back into the living room, Mark and his sawed-off were gone, and everyone was a lot less edgy. I tossed the packets of coke on the table. "Here you go. Some of the finest Colombian around."

Mike weighed the bags on Rick's scale then handed me two thick envelopes. "That's four thousand. Thanks for bringin' it up here, man. Maybe next time—"

"Next time, let's see what we can do about increasing the quantity. Make it worth my time to come up here, know what I mean?"

"If this sells as good as I think it's gonna, shouldn't have any problem buyin' more next time. Maybe I could meet you halfway somewhere?"

"Good idea. You don't think I wanna come up here and see *these* two every month?" I pointed at Rick and Vanessa. "In fact, you should have to pay me extra for that."

We all laughed. That drained the rest of the tension from the room.

I looked at my watch, then clapped my hands together. "Alright then. How about those drinks? You got anything decent around here? Scotch? Before I head back to the airport?"

"You're flying back today?" Rick said.

"Today? Hell, I'm flying back in a couple of hours. Let's get hoppin' with those drinks."

"We got Jack Daniel's," Vanessa said.

"No scotch?"

She shook her head.

"Guess it'll be Jack on the rocks then. Next time, you better have a bottle of some decent scotch here for me."

"Blech! Can't stand scotch," Rick said.

"What? Boy, I'm gonna have to disown you. I love a good scotch."

"Enough about the booze, guys. Let's do a few lines. I

wanna try this stuff Rick's been ravin' about," Mike said, scooping a big chunk onto a mirror.

My pulse quickened at the sight of that cocaine chunk. It always did, no matter how many times I looked at a pile of that South American uncut. But I had to meet with my P.O. in two days. He hadn't piss-tested me for a while. I looked at my watch. If he did test me, it'd be over forty-eight hours later. Might clear my system by then. I took another sip, glanced at Mike, who was now forming lines with the powder he'd just chopped that big old chunk into. *Forty-eight hours. No, that's not enough time.*

"You all go ahead. Just whiskey for me."

Rick looked at me, his brows furrowed, mouth turned down a little.

"If I start now, I'll probably miss my flight," I chuckled.

Rick shrugged, tucked his hair behind his ears, leaned over and snorted a line.

I flew back to Miami with that $4,000 in my briefcase, hidden in a false bottom underneath the fabric backing. Didn't snort any, but I got the same high I got every time I made a successful deal. That was one of the smallest hand-to-hands I'd made, but walking through Miami International with four ounces of coke strapped to your chest, and back with all that cash, is no small feat. Takes some skill, some guts and a lot of luck.

I also enjoyed the feeling that Rick was proud, not so much of me, but about bringing some of Colombia's finest into his neighborhood. Nothing to scoff at there. And once word got out on the street in Columbus about the high quality of this blow, everyone would be coming back for more.

In hindsight, I'm not proud of getting my son into the cocaine business. Not proud at all. But I'll say this. I thought it would help him out. He'd already been dealing weed, so me sharing some of the finest cocaine in the world could only lift him up some. He was struggling so much, had no money, no decent-paying job. And he was more than willing.

It wasn't long before the truth finally came out between me and Lynn also. And after she snorted a big old line in front of me, I could tell she wasn't new to drug use. Hell, I didn't start using coke like she was at nineteen until I was in my thirties. Honestly, it took a load off my mind that I wasn't the one introducing her to drugs. And that it was finally all out in the open. She was another person I could now be myself with. That was a good thing, because she was visiting regularly now too.

I loved having my kids back in my life. They were my children, for what it was worth. Despite me not being around since they were seven and nine, they turned out more like me than I expected.

And I was damn proud of my uncut cocaine and sharing it with my children made me feel generous and fun and— full of love. The kind of love generated and intensified by cocaine, like you're about to explode.

Only problem was, when I came down, I wasn't capable of feeling anything, paternal or otherwise. When I came down, I was pretty hollow. Then, there was a kernel of doubt or uneasiness in the back of my brain, way back there, about Rick working for me and about snorting with both him and Lynn. Mostly, I pushed that thought away, put my walls up, told myself they were adults now, that what me and Rick were doing was just business.

But things got more uncomfortable over time.

What started out as a favor to Rick, me giving him some of this really good cocaine to sell, turned into a regular part of my business. He had some connections and ended up moving a lot of coke for me. Mainly, he worked with Mike, sometimes another connection, a man who went by Marlboro Man—or Lucky Strike or some nickname related to cigarettes. In no time at all, Rick was making way more money than he'd ever made selling weed.

I made a few deliveries to Rick and Mike in Ohio. Once in a while, they came down to Florida to pick up the product. As the scale of our operation grew, I couldn't keep making the deliveries myself. The last one I made, I carried just under a half-kilo, taped onto my body in various places, through security at Miami International. Then I walked back through security at the Columbus airport with $22,000, much of it also taped to my body, some stashed in my briefcase. The cash was far more difficult to hide than the drugs, because it took up so much space. You don't work in hundred-dollar bills in smuggling, too conspicuous. You work in fives, tens some twenties, the kind of cash most folks carry around. When you're talking about $22,000 in small bills, that weighs more than the coke I transported up to them. Even if I made it through with the cocaine, that amount of cash would definitely draw the attention of the police. Flying cocaine up to Rick on commercial flights was getting risky.

After we exchanged money and coke on that trip, I told them that was the last time I'd fly their merchandise up to them. Instead, we arranged to start meeting in North Carolina—in the small town where my folks lived. North Carolina was always a good halfway point, and, if I got caught, I could always tell James my folks had an emergency or needed some help, and I forgot to get his permission.

I was actually hoping Rick would slow down if he had to come and get the blow. Slow down his coke use, that is. Another one of those nagging thoughts I was trying to ignore. The problem was he started smoking the coke. That crack was some bad shit, got a person strung out fast. When I was on the force, there was no such thing as crack or smoking cocaine. Never saw crack, never heard of it. By the time I was smuggling again after my vacation, crack was everywhere.

I'd come in contact with people who were crack addicts. They may have still lived in a mansion, but I knew a crackhead when I saw one. Usually sickly-skinny, talked a mile a minute, paranoid as shit, scratching and picking at their skin, running their tongue all over their lips and inside their mouths—non-stop.

Now I wasn't selling cocaine on the streets, like people I'd arrested in the past. Guess I lucked out, because I started closer to the top: anything I sold was in kilos, never grams or ounces. And the money was so good, I never thought about that end of things, about people on the streets—junkies, teenagers. They never crossed my mind. Until I watched what happened to Rick.

The next time I saw Rick, his face was gaunt, his cheekbones sticking out. Made me sick to my stomach, the exact way I'd felt when he was a little boy and had eye surgery to correct a crossed eye. When he came out of that surgery, a thick gauze padding over his eye, I about puked. Just the thought of the surgeon cutting on his little eye. Now here he was wasting away before my eyes.

Despite Rick being a grown man, this being just business and all that, I asked a guy I knew, Leroy, to call him and try to talk some sense into him about smoking cocaine. Before Leroy went to prison at Eglin, which is where I met him, he'd lived—if you can call it living—in a Miami safehouse run by Escobar's cartel. Every room in that house was stacked with boxes of cocaine being moved out, then with boxes of cash heading back to Medellín. Leroy's job was simply to stay in that safehouse at all times and make sure no one entered the house who wasn't supposed to. That's all. That was his sole job. So, mostly what he did was sit in that safehouse and smoke cocaine, all day long, every day, waiting for the contacts to show up and make exchanges. When that smuggling ring was taken down by DEA and Leroy was arrested, he'd been smoking coke for several days in a row. Barely remembered anything until he woke up in jail.

From the look of Rick when I saw him next, Leroy's call hadn't helped at all. He was as skinny as when he was a scrawny teenager. Skin and bones. And he owed me money, which meant I owed the Colombians money. With this pure cocaine, in such large quantities, it was hard to lose money on a deal. Unless your product was stolen, confiscated by the police, cut so much that no one would buy it or you snorted most of it. Or in Rick's case, smoked most of it. That time, I'd fronted Rick two kilos, and he smoked up his profit in a few weeks. He couldn't stay away from it.

I still couldn't bring myself to cut him off. I should've; with anyone else, I would've. But he was so hooked on the stuff, I was afraid of what he'd do to feed his addiction if he wasn't getting it from me. And he needed to earn that money back.

That was some real bad business from any angle. After that, whenever Rick wanted to move some product, I limited how much I fronted him—no more than a quarter-kilo at a time. What else could I do?

I kept telling myself I needed to stop using with my kids and working with Rick. That promise, though, was like trying to quit cocaine at the end of the day. No matter how much I promised myself I was snorting my last line, I kept going back for more. I'd snort until my stash was gone, or I hit a physical wall from lack of sleep and food and finally just crashed.

My thinking was similar with my kids. Every time I used with one of them, I told myself that was the last time. But when they showed up again looking for cocaine, I handed it right over. And I was usually flying on that pure Colombian, that euphoria making everything alright. All that other stuff: uncomfortable feelings, guilt, my conscience—poof! It all disappeared.

CHAPTER 21
THE WIND IN THE DARK

As my smuggling career took off, I found a bigger, much nicer apartment, which I rented under an alias. Kept my first apartment too, which was in my real name. That's the one James knew about and where I lived. The other one was my smuggling apartment, just like in the old days. This one is where I stashed my smuggling paraphernalia: false IDs, locking jewelry cases for our increasingly larger runs of cocaine and lots and lots of cash —stuffed everywhere. I stuffed cash in suitcases, safe-deposit boxes all over town, even in the cushions of a couch.

After we completed several cocaine deals, Roger and I started talking about scaling up. Gustavo was out of prison by this time and suggested I might want to work directly with his family in Medellín. I liked the sound of that. He trusted me enough to invite me into his world there. And we could make greater profits.

Everyone who touched the cocaine took a piece of the

profit, so if we got our product direct from South America, we made more money.

Gustavo said he could sell us thirty kilos for about $100,000; the more we bought, the better the deal. We could sell that in the States for over a million dollars.

All we needed was a plane and a pilot. This time, we had our own money.

Roger and I sat across from each other at his mahogany dining table discussing planes one evening. As he talked, I noticed that Maureen kept that table so well-polished that I could see our scotch glasses reflected in the table's surface. *Classy. She's one classy lady.*

"If we get a big plane, we can bring in bigger loads and make it to South America without refueling. We wouldn't have to fly over as often," Roger said, sipping his scotch.

"I'd rather keep our operations small. If we bring in small loads, we'll only need a few people. We'll know what two or three other people are doing; we can see it. Keeps things manageable that way. Smaller plane costs less. I can get us a Twin Beech for a couple hundred thousand. It'll carry any amount of coke we ever wanna buy. If we get a good pilot, he can fly it solo. So we only need to add one new person."

"Yeah, but can we get back and forth to Colombia in a Twin Beech without refueling?"

"Nope. We have to refuel in the Bahamas."

He shook his head. "Sounds risky."

I exhaled smoke and crushed my cigarette out, the ashtray rattling on the tabletop. "I know a guy, Curt, flies through the Bahamas. He knows some of the cops down there. I'll give him a ring, see what we can cook up. Just gotta find the right cops and pay them enough. They look the other way. There's not much risk for them. They're paid in cash, so there's no way to link them to a plane if a pilot does get arrested. If the money's good enough, they can't pass it up."

Before long, Roger and I were sitting in the Bahamas at an open-air restaurant overlooking the milky blue-green waters of a harbor. I'd just visited James that morning and pissed what I was sure was a clean test, so I didn't have a care in the world. I was enjoying my scotch on the rocks, some mellow reggae music and some foxy ladies in very skimpy bikinis. A warm breeze brushed the tablecloth against my leg. I glanced down to make sure no one was messing with my duffle bag, which contained $50,000 cash. Roger looked at his watch again.

A pudgy man who fit the description Curt had given me sauntered onto the patio, scanning the tables. I watched him searching for the black bag at my feet. When he noticed it, he made eye contact and walked to our table. I tipped my chin up in a small nod to him.

"Are you Mr. Wilson?" he asked. My usual cover name.

"That's me. You Edward?" We all shook hands and introduced ourselves. Edward glanced at the empty tables surrounding us. He set his sunglasses on the table and ordered a beer.

"We sure appreciate your time, and Curt sends his regards. If you don't mind, we'll get right down to business," I said.

Edward nodded. He already had rings of sweat soaking through his shirt.

I leaned forward. "We need a place to store some fuel for

our airplane. We'd like to have four, five hundred gallons not far from an airstrip—"

"How long of a runway? What kind of plane?"

"Fifteen hundred feet. It's a small plane. A Twin Beech," Roger said.

Just then, the waitress came to our table. "You all ready to order?"

"Gin and tonic," Edward said.

Roger shook his head. "We'll wait on dinner for now."

Edward watched her walk away then looked around at the nearby tables again. "This won't be cheap. In the Bahamas, you have to pay for more than the fuel. We have to find a runway, haul the barrels there—"

I wrote "$50,000" on a napkin and slid it to him.

He glanced at the napkin, nodded. "When is your next trip?"

"Around mid-March."

The waitress returned with his gin and tonic. After she left again, Edward spread a map out on the table, circled an area and drew an X near what looked like an open field then slid it between Roger and me. We looked at the map, then nodded at each other.

Roger folded the map. "Looks like a good strip."

Edward scribbled a phone number on the map. "Call me end of February, before you fly, to make sure everything's all set up. And the day before you fly into the Bahamas. Always good to check with me then."

I tapped on the napkin. "With this payment, we'd expect nothin' to go wrong, especially the day before we land here."

"No, should be fine. But, just in case—"

Roger looked back and forth between Edward and me. "In case of what?"

"Maybe we have to change the location of the strip or the fuel. Only to protect your investment. In case someone found it. Understand?"

"And this is the only phone number you have?" I pointed at the number on the map. "We can reach you here anytime?"

"Anytime."

"And you've got our number," Roger said. "So if anything changes, you let us know. As soon as possible."

"I will," Edward said. "And nothing personal, but I want to go count the money before you leave."

I glanced down at my duffle bag. "No problem. Take all the time you need."

He took the bag and headed to the restroom. When he came back, we all shook hands and Edward hurried from the restaurant.

"Did we just kiss fifty grand good-bye?" Roger asked.

"Curt says these cops'll do anything for the right amount of money. And fifty grand is more than the right amount."

He puffed his cheeks out with a big exhale. "I s'pose. I still say, a bigger plane, and we won't need this fuel stop."

"You gettin' old and cranky on me? It's gonna be fine. And look at where we are." I gestured to the beach with all the ladies in bikinis. "Besides, Curt recommended Edward. And I trust Curt. That's all that matters, right?"

"If you say so."

Another breeze blew in from the sea. The warm air reminded me of those sweaty, dark nights years ago, unloading hundreds of bales of marijuana while mosquitos were eating me alive. How good a little breeze would feel. I thought about my first botched deal with that snitch Karen, the Quaaludes, finally smuggling large quantities of marijuana, then cocaine. Coke was so much easier to move— smaller volumes but worth so much more than weed. If I needed to, I could move cocaine in the light of day. Just throw a dozen kilos in the trunk and drive it to a distributor.

Everything about smuggling cocaine was classier than my early smuggling days. Then I recalled that perfect Thanksgiving day when I was able to use cocaine like a gentleman. That gentleman was how I saw myself now: in charge of my world, at the top of my game.

I wondered if trusting my instincts and the people I worked with was all that mattered. Sitting there on the Caribbean Sea, my future stretched out ahead of me like a promise. If I wanted to maintain my success, I needed far more than trust and instincts. I had to be like the breeze on one of those dark nights, had to move through and around everyone and everything. Might be able to hear the wind move through the trees in the dark, but you could never see it. I needed to be like that, going wherever I wanted to but always unseen. Like the wind in the dark.

CHAPTER 22
OUT OF CONTROL

Back in the States, Roger, Jack and I ramped up our operations. We partnered with a colleague of Roger's who went by the name of Curly. Pretty funny since he was as bald as a bowling ball. Curly had flown some operations for Larry back when Roger was still working for Larry. All they needed was a guy who went by Moe, and they could call themselves The Three Stooges. I'd managed to avoid Larry since my vacation ended and planned to continue doing so, but if Roger said Curly was cool, I wasn't questioning his judgment. Even if he was one of The Three Stooges.

The four of us pooled together over $500,000 to buy a Twin Beech and thirty kilos direct from Gustavo in Medellín. The time and risk to fly down there was only worth it if we came back with at least thirty kilos. And we had to pay up front. They wouldn't give us that much cocaine on the arm. Even though they knew we always paid, they'd be crazy to let us leave the country with that much and hope we came back later to pay for it. Too many things could go wrong.

Curly touched the plane down pretty damn well on a crude dirt airstrip in the jungle outside of Medellín. As Curly cut the engines, Nico jumped out of the plane and exchanged sideways hugs and backslaps with Gustavo. Three other men stood at the edge of the clearing, holding automatic rifles at the ready, scanning the perimeter of the runway and the dense jungle just beyond. Curly and I made eye contact with each other. He pulled a thirty-eight pistol from a compartment and slid it in his pocket. My pistol was in my ankle holster and my nine-millimeter was in my briefcase.

My body was tense as I climbed out of the plane. I reminded myself that I knew what I was doing, had done this dozens of times.

Introductions were made, with Gustavo translating. I was glad everybody else was sweating in the humidity too. As we loaded into two nearby Jeeps, the plane engines now quiet, the jungle come back to life, birds and animals squawking and screeching all around us.

We drove ten, maybe fifteen minutes on dirt roads, then pulled into a compound of what looked like basic concrete buildings, but pretty new-looking ones. Very few windows or doors. Men with assault rifles all around. No doubt this was where the merchandise was kept.

Inside, Rafael sat behind a big desk. These cocaine operations truly were family-run. Workers in the jungles all over South America were cooking cocaine, but at the upper echelons, families ran the operations. Rafael was having a smoke, his feet propped up on the desk, like this was a used-car lot or something. Guess all those AK-47s put him at ease. They made me nervous as hell.

We all talked, Curly gave them our briefcase of money and they invited us into a back room. The room was full—wall-to-wall, floor-to-ceiling—with kilos of cocaine, all wrapped, taped and stamped. The sight of that much product sent a bolt of adrenaline through me and got my mouth salivating. They loaded our thirty kilos into the back of the Jeep and took us back to our plane.

When you had a relationship with the Colombians, had their confidence, an exchange was that easy. Not just anybody could waltz into a Medellín cocaine distribution—what would I call it—warehouse, and walk right back out with thirty kilos. That kind of trust took years to build.

They even invited us to have lunch. As much as I would've loved to eat with them, being in the Colombian jungle with all that product and dozens of men standing around with AK-47s didn't do much for my appetite. Both Curly and I wanted to get back in the air, on our way to the Bahamas.

Now I was making close to $200,000 on each run. Part of our profit from each run was used to pay for the next Bahama fuel purchase and the next load of cocaine. Our strategy for keeping things manageable was to bring in only small loads like this. Even when we really got rolling, we didn't try to expand much, maybe forty kilos if we had the cash, and Jack and Farmer John had the buyers stateside. Mike bought at least a kilo every month. We wanted to keep things under control. But "control" and "smuggling" are words that don't go together that well. Not for long.

What money I didn't use for the next deal, I spent or

stuffed into more and more hiding places around my cover apartment or had Suzy spend it. That woman could spend. We ate out just about every night at the nicest restaurants in Miami, I bought her whatever she wanted, we took cruises to the Bahamas. Wherever we went, Suzy and I stayed at expensive hotels, suites overlooking the ocean, fully stocked wet bars, Jacuzzis. We were having a blast. That woman could party too. That's what we did: spend money and party.

This was the one difference about my smuggling this time around—cocaine use. I snorted huge quantities. Sometimes I snorted a thousand dollars' worth a day. I'm talking a thousand dollars in street value. But we had so much pure cocaine, that didn't seem like much. And I never let my drug use affect my work. Those were the best and worst of times for me. I was tight with so many Colombians and was moving more cocaine than ever. I made tons of money, but my snorting was unchecked. If only I could've used cocaine like that one Thanksgiving day. But usually, that first line of the day always did me in, had me coming back for more all day long. Then that Thanksgiving gentleman would be nowhere in sight. That perfect day was long gone now. My cocaine use was wide open. *I* was wide open. Wide open and out of control.

For the first time in several months, Gustavo's family didn't have any cocaine. One of their main suppliers had been raided and their lab shut down, and another of their distributors just took a huge load, a hundred kilos. They offered to introduce us to another connection who always had plenty.

When Gustavo introduced us and talked to this guy about us, I caught some key words that gave me the gist of what he was saying—"de confianza" and "buen dinero"— they trusted us, we had good money. Two of the reasons we'd come that far. And I was pretty sure we were going even farther today, farther into Escobar's cartel.

That fact gave me pause. By this time, in the mid-80s, Pablo Escobar ran pretty much everything in the Colombian cocaine trade. He was sending thousands of kilos to the United States every month and used an army of smugglers to do it. And I thought *I* was a badass because I was distributing twenty, thirty kilos a month.

We didn't want to go home empty-handed, but working directly with one of Escobar's men was serious business. If we didn't live up to their expectations, or anything even appeared suspicious, we'd get whacked. Escobar had been a bad dude when I was in law enforcement, and he'd gotten a lot worse since then.

While Gustavo's connection made a few phone calls, I ran through each step that had led us to this point. There were no red flags for me, and we were clearly not setting off any alarms for them either, a strong indication of our reputation. I was extremely proud of that. They didn't bring just any smuggler from Miami this deep into the Medellín cartel. And we needed some product. So, when he said he'd take us to get some coca, we moved on up to the next level. And it wasn't like we were going to be buying direct from Escobar, though I will confess, some part of me hoped we would at least meet him.

Pablo Escobar was a legend. Brutal, yes, but still a legend. Almost single-handedly, he created a multi-national drug trafficking network. And I was smack-dab in the middle of that network, or at least near the middle. Without question, I was benefitting from Escobar's cartel. Coming face-to-face with him was an opportunity most smugglers would've considered an honor.

Curly and I got in the backseat, where I promptly popped two antacids in my mouth. The further this man drove into the city, the more I wished we could stop for a few minutes. This was all happening way too fast. I needed to clear my head; would've done anything for a scotch. No cocaine, though. Definitely no blow today. Luckily, Gustavo climbed in the front. At least we wouldn't be driving around in Medellín with a complete stranger.

We drove for maybe forty minutes before pulling into a parking garage under what looked like an office building. Except for the guards, each holding AK-47 assault rifles, on some of the balconies. Nobody we'd meet here could possibly know me or my history, but my stomach tightened with nausea at the sight of those AK-47s. Escobar's men wouldn't hesitate to put a bullet right through the brain of a narc. No turning back now though. I couldn't say or do anything that would raise doubts that I was truly a Miami smuggler.

When we got out of the car, I mumbled to Gustavo. "This Escobar's place?"

He nodded. "One of them. It's fine. He won't meet with us. He's too busy, but his men can sell you some product."

Curly was sort of glaring at me out of the corner of his eye, scared shitless too, I'm sure.

As we waited in a front office, a couple of guys sauntered in, chatting in Spanish, and offered us a few lines of cocaine.

Gustavo shook his head.

Curly put his hand in front of him and said, "No, gracias."

I shook my head also. "No lo toco."

The successful Colombian drug traffickers, for the most part, didn't use the stuff. They considered smugglers who used drugs to be scumbags. Drugs screw up your thinking, and thinking straight is crucial to running a smuggling operation. And in case we actually came face-to-face with Escobar, I wanted to be thinking clearly, very clearly.

I tried to remain aloof and relaxed while guards with submachine guns stood at the doorway to another room. Leaning back in my chair, I smoked a cigarette and took in the room. The furniture looked European, old-style: chairs made of dark, carved wood and plush upholstery; lamps with ornate, stained-glass lampshades; sterling-silver coffee pot and tray; even the ashtrays looked like silver. We'd entered into a circle of power. And a circle of no mistakes. Not with those two mini-Uzis right in front of us.

A guard came through the closed door so abruptly that I flinched, hopefully, not noticeably. "Entrar," he said, looking at the guards and ticking his head back to the door he'd just walked through. The two guards motioned us into the room.

There have been a few times in my life where I felt truly frightened. Walking into that next room was one of those moments. A shiver ran up my spine and into the base of my skull, making it feel like the hair on my neck stood on end.

Sitting at a desk, right in front of us, was the man who had created a cocaine empire in only a handful of years, the man against who I'd helped wage a war, the man all of my cocaine came from.

Even Gustavo looked surprised. And nervous. It occurred to me then, he perhaps had more to lose than me. If he brought two Americanos this far into the cartel and things went wrong, he'd be held responsible.

"Don Pablo," Gustavo said, shaking his hand. "Muchas gracias por su tiempo."

Pablo Escobar swept his arm towards some chairs and said, "Sit. Por favor." He began talking in Spanish, and Gustavo translated. He asked us how we ran our business and how we liked to be paid, in cash or cocaine. This question made me nervous because it didn't sound like he was talking about selling us cocaine, he was talking about us working for him. How could I explain to him that we weren't looking for work, just a few kilos of coke? Hopefully Gustavo was explaining all of that.

The door opened without a sound and an older woman carried in a tray of coffee and pastries, setting it on a coffee table in front of us. She then put one of the cups and a pastry in front of Pablo. He took a sip and gestured for us to do the same. My stomach was burning, but I wasn't about to refuse his offer of food and drink. I poured a hefty amount of milk into my coffee and took a bite of pastry, more of a crunchy coconut cookie, while Pablo clarified that if we were to work together, we would need to run operations his way, to follow his orders. We were all clear who would be in charge, no doubt about that. He was looking for pilots with their own planes who could move at least a hundred and fifty kilos of cocaine a week.

I looked at Curly and felt the sting of perspiration break out under my arms. In my head, I calculated that amount into dollars—over four million in profit. I was flattered just to be in this place—flattered and frightened. Here I was, breaking bread and talking business with the biggest drug lord in the world. But there was no way in hell we could move a hundred and fifty kilos. I didn't even want to do business at that level. Talk about unmanageable. Smugglers who worked at that scale usually ended up in prison or dead, and I didn't plan on either of those happening to me right now. I was still looking at more than a year of parole and wasn't about to try hiding operations that involved hundreds of kilos each week. That would be insane.

Not many people made it into that circle of power. But to be there at the level I was at, so inadequate that I couldn't even move his minimum, I felt out of place. "Gustavo, please tell Don Pablo it'd be an honor to work for him, but to be honest, it'd put a lotta pressure on us to move that much cocaine. And we'd never commit to somethin' we couldn't deliver on. But we'd love to purchase thirty kilos today, if that's possible."

Amazingly, we left South America with thirty kilos and an option for more, way more, if and when we were ready to move it. While the cocaine we'd been getting for the past year was ultimately from Escobar's operations, I wanted to keep more than a few arm's lengths between him and us. Just to be safe, given my history.

Curly and I were pretty quiet on the drive back to our plane. Quiet as we took off with thirty kilos. I chewed on

Rolaids and watched the landscape below us. From that altitude, Medellín looked like a gray, concrete scab surrounded by a forest of green. Only when the city was no longer visible did we each snort a few pinches of the cocaine. All the adrenaline now gone, and buzzing from the blow, we talked about what had just transpired.

"Holy fuck! I thought I was gonna shit my pants when I saw Escobar sittin' there," Curly said.

"No kiddin'. He's one scary dude."

"And in the future, I'll just wait in a hotel 'til you come back with the product."

"What, no more jungle rides for you?" We both laughed.

"Least we came away with some good stuff."

"Yep. Farmer John's not gonna have any trouble selling this load."

We followed the mountains north of Medellín for an hour, then the mountains petered out into the green plains on the north coast of Colombia. Then finally there was the blue-green of the Caribbean Sea, the white line of surf along the coast. We were officially out of South America. I could breathe easier. My stomach stopped burning, probably from the antacids, but I like to think it was from the sight of the ocean. Some of my best days were spent on the ocean: in Hawaii when Rick was a newborn, sailing the Keys with Carl and our families, in the Marines at Guantanamo Bay. In fact, our flight to the Bahamas would take us near Guantanamo Naval Base, at least as the crow flies or, in our case, the Twin Beech.

The first place I'd been stationed after boot camp was Guantanamo Bay, right after the Bay of Pigs invasion. Tensions were really high between U.S., Cuba and Russia, so things were exciting for us Marines. I kept my eyes and ears open and excelled, advancing to a Corporal E-4 before anyone else in my platoon. The Navy base and surrounding community were pretty basic. Not a lot to do in our free time except drink, play poker and write letters, if you were lucky enough to have a sweetheart (which I was—I'd just started writing to Linda, who was in nursing school with my sister). We did training exercises in the hills surrounding us, which were dry, hot and barren with very few trees—made for some scorching maneuvers. But the Caribbean Sea was like nothing I'd ever seen or heard or smelled before. Here I was, more than two decades later, looking out over that amazing water again.

So much had happened in those twenty years: four years in the Marines, a wife, a family (a second wife, a second family), an exciting career as a policeman. My life had taken some crazy, unexpected turns too. After all, I'd planned to be a preacher; could've never predicted I'd become a smuggler. Or go to prison. Or use drugs with my kids. And I never thought, in a million years, that I—me, a former undercover narcotics agent—would purchase thirty kilos of cocaine direct from Pablo Escobar.

Lots of twists and turns. As usual, I was just going along for the ride.

CHAPTER 23
PLAIN OL' LUCK

Every run we made was different: different amounts of product, different wholesale and street prices, bad weather, good weather and now the Bahama-refuel variable. Some runs went well, some not so well.

That line of work isn't exactly full of honest people. One of my worst days smuggling, Gustavo's family fronted me a couple kilos to show to a potential distributor. This guy, can't even remember his name, was down on his luck. This would've given him a good boost; he could've made a lot of money and got more product the next month. Instead, he blew it—all of it. Told me he could move it but never came back with the money. I hated to do it, but I had to go to the Colombians and tell them what happened. I didn't have the money to pay them right then, so I was up front and honest about it. It was awful. I didn't know what they'd do. Try to whack me or, at least, I thought I'd lose their confidence, their business. But they let me make good on it. I eventually paid them back.

I'm proud to say in all the years I worked with the

Colombians, I never took anything I couldn't get rid of, never said I could move stuff when I couldn't, never stole anyone's stuff, and I always paid for drugs that were fronted to me. And that honesty paid off, because I was highly trusted by the Colombians. I asked for all the cocaine I ever wanted, always got it and they never lost a penny. I, on the other hand, lost more than a few pennies over the years.

On one run, something went bad in the Bahamas. The cops there had been paid off, fuel was purchased and we just bought our product in Colombia. When we landed in the islands, our fuel wasn't there. Only the police. They didn't arrest us, just confiscated our plane—with all of our product. That's all they wanted. Wasn't anything we could do. Couldn't call the cops. They were the ones who took our stuff. And even if it had been other smugglers, you can't report stolen cocaine.

We had to find a new contact in the Bahamas, locate a new runway, buy a new plane, everything. I lost a lot of money on that run.

That money, drug money, is never really free and clear. Part of the money you make on each run is used for the next one, for the product, the supplies, the fuel, hotels, rental cars. And lots of that money went right up my nose.

By this time, I hardly went more than a few days without snorting cocaine, and when I did, I snorted large quantities. Why I never failed a urine test is beyond me.

I always stopped snorting five days before visiting my P.O. Then I walked into his office, smiling, and said, "Hurry up and get me that sample cup. I drank a whole pot of coffee this mornin'." Over time, that seemed to minimize his interest in requesting urine samples, or maybe after the first few came back negative, he figured I was straight. Or maybe he just hated his job so much, working for probably $20,000 a year, that he didn't give a shit anymore. All he wanted to do was go fishing in the Keys.

Had a few close calls when my P.O. called me in for an unscheduled visit, which usually meant a urine test. Once, I'd snorted a few days prior to one of these random tests, and I understood that cocaine could show up in the urine up to three days later, sometimes five. Just like when I was a policeman, I imagined that James relied on his instincts and my attitude to determine whether I was bullshitting him. Since I didn't have any choice, I acted all happy to see him and unconcerned about taking a piss test. Then for twenty-four hours, I was terrified I was going back to prison. But I never heard back from him. The sample came back clean, or based on my willingness to provide it, he never sent it to the lab.

The worst interaction with James happened one morning when I'd been up all night, snorting. It was about nine in the morning. I was finally coming down from the coke enough to try to sleep when I heard a knock on my door. My car was parked out front, so I couldn't pretend to be gone. I shoved my stash of coke in a gym bag in the back of my closet, hustled to the bathroom and splashed cold water on my face.

Another louder knock. "Just a minute," I hollered. I splashed water all over my hair, then I blew my nose and checked it in the mirror for any bloody snot. I took my shirt off and threw the damp towel around my neck.

More knocking.

"I'm coming! Hold your horses." I opened the door to find James standing there. "Hey, man. Sorry about that. Was just gettin' outta the shower. Come on in."

Running the towel over my hair, I wiped off the beads of sweat that I could feel forming on my temples.

"Was in the neighborhood and thought I'd stop in."

Heading into the kitchen, I said, "I'm gonna get myself a glass of milk. Haven't had breakfast yet. Get you some-thin'?" In the kitchen, I slipped a few Rolaids into my mouth then poured a glass of milk.

"Got any coffee?"

"Sorry. All out." I intended to keep this visit short. Apparently he didn't. He was dropping down in the sofa.

James scanned the apartment then looked down and rubbed the leather upholstery. "Getting some nice furniture in this place, huh? Car-polishing business must be doing good."

"Yeah, business *is* good. Folks like their cars shiny in Miami. I'm meetin' all kinds of new people. Get some nice tips from businessmen, especially the ones with Mercedes and BMWs. Keeps me outta trouble and nice to make an honest living for a change." *Okay, stop talking so much.*

Paranoid from snorting all night, I couldn't think straight. Unable to avoid him any longer, I sat down across from him hoping my pupils weren't huge. I reminded myself that I knew how to snow people, had been fooling people for years. Then, another part of me—no, like another person—took over the conversation. My pulse slowed, I lit a cigarette, casually chatted with him like I didn't have a care in the world. Joked with him a little, trying to make him laugh, which wasn't easy.

"You ready to get that filthy car of yours detailed? Give you the parolee discount. Have that thing shiny on the outside and smellin' good inside. Good enough to take your wife out to dinner in it."

He waved me away. "Nah."

"What? You don't take your wife to dinner? Or you take her in your stinky old car?"

"Neither. Just don't want a polish today. Just stopping by to check on you."

"Well, sure appreciate it. Need me downtown for a sample?" God, let his answer be no.

"Don't think so. Catch you next time."

When he finally left half an hour later, the sun poured through the door, and I could see the usual haze of humidity forming in the distance. I collapsed on the sofa for several minutes, wondering if I'd ever fall asleep between being all coked up and the jolt of James' unplanned visit. Maybe I should leave Miami, I thought. Get away from all this cocaine.

After that scare with James, I thought about leaving Miami more and more often. If I could get the hell away from that city, away from the state, I'd have to give up the smuggling. If I did that, I'd naturally quit using coke.

But we had such a lucrative arrangement with Gustavo's family that I just couldn't walk away from it. When I was high on cocaine, I loved all the power and prestige, the ecstasy, the money, my reputation with the Colombians. I felt like I could go on smuggling for years. My plans made perfect sense.

When I came down, I saw the insanity of my smuggling: sneaking around my P.O., always watching over my shoulder and knowing, in my bones, that my smuggling career wasn't going to end pretty.

But the smuggling and uncut Colombian kept winning out. Walking away would've taken more energy and strength than continuing. I simply couldn't walk away from the thrill and excitement and euphoria and the money—so much money.

A little over a year into our smuggling operation, this drug smuggler, Donnie's, car got blown up—with him inside it. We'd partnered with Donnie on a recent operation. He was a nice-enough guy, but I don't think he enjoyed smuggling as much as he just liked drugs. He wasn't too savvy, and he floated around working with different smugglers here and there, not just our group. Word was that he'd been arrested with some marijuana, enough that the DEA got him to talk. Apparently, he was turning over evidence about other smugglers to avoid prison. That kind of shit doesn't go over well in the criminal world. No one tolerates a snitch, not for long. So, I wasn't surprised he got whacked.

Then James showed up on my doorstep with a DEA agent questioning me about Donnie and what I knew about him. They were drilling me. Did I know him? How did I know him? Had I worked with him? Before prison or after? Did I know any of these other men? What kind of work had I done on that dynamite blasting crew in North Carolina? Where was I the night he was killed?

"Whoa, whoa, whoa. Wait a minute, man. What's goin' on here?" I said to the agent.

"Just checking our facts."

"Yeah, I knew Donnie. He was a customer. I detailed his car every month. And I was right here"—I pointed at the floor under my feet—"with Suzy that night. As far as my experience with dynamite, I drove a truck for that blasting crew. Never touched the explosives. Don't know the first thing about 'em."

"Donnie told us he'd been working with you and a few other men. Smuggling co—"

"Hold on there." My hands shot up, palms facing the agent. "Am I being charged with somethin' here? Cuz if I am, I want my attorney present."

The DEA agent said, "We're just starting an investigation, and there's a lot pointing at you. Donnie told us you haven't kept your nose clean."

That son of a bitch ratted us out. If Donnie, their witness, was now dead, there wasn't shit pointing at me. I knew what the DEA was up to: intimidating a suspect, making you think they had the goods on you so you'd confess. After hearing Donnie had ratted on us, I was glad someone whacked him.

"You gonna read me my rights here or what? I just polished the man's car. Don't know nothin' about any explosion." I looked at James, then back to the agent. "And I've had clean piss tests since I got outta the pen. Got a great job. So I don't know what you think's pointin' at me, but if you wanna keep on here, I want my attorney present."

"We'll be watching you," the agent said, pointing at me.

I raised my eyebrows. "Isn't that what my POs been

doing for the past year and half? Don't recall having any violations."

James shook his head. "Nope, none."

"Well, DEA's keeping an eye on you too."

I sat tight for a few weeks after that, didn't make any runs, stayed away from everybody. Never heard back from the DEA. They never filed any charges against me. But this was going to be the end of my smuggling. It had to be. I couldn't keep on, not with the DEA all over my ass now.

That same week, Roger told me he wanted out. Maureen was threatening to leave him if he didn't quit. Her doctor told her recently she had a perforated septum that required surgery to repair. Then hearing about my DEA visit had been the last straw for her. They'd run out of ways to launder and hide all the cash they were raking in, and she was freaked out that the DEA would start snooping around their "businesses."

When Maureen and Roger invited me to dinner, I never thought that would be the last time I saw them. Funny thing about partners in crime, even if you really like someone—God knows you spend enough time with them, sometimes in highly stressful situations, seeing a side of each other no one else ever sees—once your time together is over, it's over. You aren't really friends, just business associates.

I still had my connections to Gustavo, Nico and Javi and all their cocaine. But losing my main partner, and access to Curly and his plane, took the wind out of my sails. Starting up with a new partner took so much energy, figuring out who you can trust, then if you found someone, finding out who they worked with. Every person in a smuggling ring introduced another risk—another potential snitch or undercover narc or informant or just a loose cannon who could screw everything up with one bad decision. I just wasn't up for starting over. And with DEA breathing down my neck, it was time to quit.

During my next visit with James, he told me to think about transferring out of Miami, preferably out of state. Said he'd put in the paperwork, if I put in a request for some place I could make a new start. That, or he was recommending a transfer.

Just like that, my smuggling career was coming to an end. Leaving Miami would seal the deal. I dreaded the idea of going back to selling cars, but there wasn't anything I could do about it. This was one of those decisions that life made for me. Or, in this case, the parole office.

Before I could transfer my parole to another state, I needed a plan for where I'd live and work. What made the most sense was to move back to where my parents had retired, where Laura and I'd lived after I resigned from Dade County. Figured the parole departments in both Florida and North Carolina would look favorably on that, having a place to land and family support. And my folks were getting older, could use my help sometimes. I wasn't mowing any lawns, but I sure could pay some kid to do it.

I didn't think the idea of a car-detailing business in small-town North Carolina would fly though. Miami, sure, but North Carolina? No. My father had been talking to me since he retired about how popular antiques were in the Carolinas, how auction houses would be packed every weekend and how good I'd be at that business. Some of those auction companies made good money, buying old furniture that folks didn't even know were worth much, polishing them up and selling them for a good little profit.

So, when I filled out my transfer request, that was my plan: to open an antique auction company. I believed that plan.

CHAPTER 24
OUT OF MIAMI, AGAIN

That fall, my parole supervision was transferred to North Carolina, and I moved there with my car, several suitcases full of cash and a plan to start a new business, a new life. I gave everything else in my apartment to Suzy; walked away from her like I did with anyone. Those walls just went up, and I was gone. She was pissed that I was taking off, just like that—demonstrated with a snap of her fingers. I told her she could come up and visit if she wanted. But I warned her, I was leaving that nose candy behind.

My folks wanted me to stay with them until I found a place. A forty-four-year-old parolee living with his parents? Definitely not the image I wanted for myself. I stayed in a hotel until I found an apartment.

My new P.O., Lloyd, loved the antique business and thought I made a good decision to start an auction company. He told me that he wanted to get into antiques when he retired, which looked to be about any day now.

That old man wasn't moving too fast anymore and didn't care to.

As I scouted around the auction businesses in town, I met this guy, Marvin, who spoke with a thick Southern drawl and was a pro auctioneer. He called an auction so fast I could barely understand what he was saying, and he'd keep that pace up for hours. After a few meetings, he took me up on my offer to go into business together.

We purchased a sprawling metal building on the outskirts of town. We sold some antiques and a lot of junk at first. To draw bigger crowds, we started inviting gospel singers from local churches to perform there for an hour before the auctions began. That filled our seats, and some nights we had four hundred of them out on the floor.

My life quickly became normal: I popped over to my parents for Sunday dinners, took them out for dinner on Wednesdays, scouted for antiques during the week, worked the auctions on Friday and Saturday nights, even started seeing some women. Suzy drove up once to visit me before realizing I wasn't serious enough to keep our relationship going long-distance. Hell, Lloyd wasn't letting me go back down to Miami every month, and if I snuck down there, it'd only be for one thing. And it wasn't a woman.

Marvin and his wife fixed me up with a local gal and when I picked her up, she came out carrying a bulky, scraped-up, worn-out leather purse.

"Uh, we can't go out in public like that," I said, pointing at her purse. "That thing looks like a damn saddle bag."

She chuckled a little until she realized I wasn't kidding, then her mouth fell open slightly. "I love this purse. I've had it for years."

"Yeah, I can tell. C'mon, we're goin' to the mall first."

I insisted she buy a new purse before I took her to the 30th Edition, the fanciest restaurant in Charlotte. At the mall, I was pointing at the leather Guccis, but she peeked at the price tags then strolled over to the cheap purses. I rolled my eyes and nudged her back to the Guccis. She refused. Oh, this is gonna be a great evening, I thought. Anything would be an improvement over that hulking saddle bag, even the cheap $50 purse she finally let me purchase.

At dinner we were looking over the menu, and she leaned close and whispered, "John, what is this item?" She pointed at the filet mignon.

Oh, yes, a lovely evening. Suzy, and my ex-wife Laura, would've ordered filet mignon without even looking at a menu. Linda, she was more of a lobster lady, but she definitely knew what filet mignon was. By this time, I was used to wining and dining women who appreciated, even expected, as much. I prided myself on knowing how to romance a lady, but I think I was a bit much for this small-town gal. Turned out she was wild in the sack though, so we dated for a couple of months.

While my life may have looked normal from the outside, inside, nothing was normal. Without the stimulation of smuggling and cocaine, everything was stagnant. I was simply going through the motions of life. The auction business wasn't bad; it just wasn't exciting, and I was running out of money, fast. At least the amount I was used to.

On top of feeling listless and bored, thoughts about getting cocaine into Charlotte, the nearest big city, up to Rick (still only small quantities unless he paid upfront) and his associate Mike, started popping into my brain. For weeks, I vacillated, back and forth, back and forth. Obsessively. I ignored the thoughts about smuggling, then nurtured them, assessing everyone I met as a potential distributor. I focused on building my new auction business, then developed elaborate smuggling plans. How could I get product up here? Where could I stash it? How many kilos could I move and how fast? I drank enough scotch to shut my brain up, then drank so much it fueled my smuggling fantasies.

But my situation was completely different now. For one, Charlotte sure as hell wasn't Miami; the city wasn't swarming with smugglers. Flying under the radar, being invisible, would be much more difficult here. Two, Lloyd's caseload was maybe a dozen parolees, compared to James who had a few dozen. Driving while on parole from Miami to Atlanta with a load of cocaine for Farmer John was no small feat. Driving from a dinky town in North Carolina to Miami and back with a dozen or so kilos was bordering on … insanity.

After several weeks of obsessing about smuggling again, I took Marvin out for a full-on barbecue dinner. That doesn't sound fancy, but North Carolina barbecue is, by far, the best in the world. Marvin was a savvy businessman, so he didn't take much convincing to expand our business once I described the amount of money he stood to earn by letting me use the auction barn for my Miami-based business. The auction company would be used simply to launder the money and, on occasion, briefly store some of my merchandise. I told him not to worry, my merchandise wouldn't take up any floor space. Assured him that, in fact, he'd never see my product—plausible deniability. He didn't want to know any more, and we agreed on terms, mainly financial ones. If you pay people enough, and you give them deniability, you can find all kinds of willing partners.

Rick and Mike were more than happy to drive to North Carolina to pick up a package, as it was ten hours closer to them than Miami. They could make it, round-trip, in one day. No more staying in hotels, which was always trouble when you're hauling a kilo of uncut cocaine. Chances are you're not sleeping anyways, but driving from Columbus, Ohio to Miami without staying overnight somewhere must have been a bitch. That's why I'd always flown. I left the two-day drives to the young'uns.

For the Charlotte distribution, I identified a few people I figured were involved with drugs—I did that without even thinking, an instinct I'd honed over the past fifteen years on both sides. My initial list of definites: the twenty-something lady who cleaned my apartment and my real estate agent, Bill.

Before long, I was talking with Javi in Miami again. He agreed to drive some stuff up to me. Just like that, with only a phone call. I was off and running again. Man, did it feel good, so good, I never looked back. Not even a glance. No more wavering, no more bouncing back and forth between *my* normal life and *a* normal life, no more questioning if I should or shouldn't. Just full speed ahead.

Within a week, I was in possession of a few kilos. This stuff came from a different family in Colombia; I could tell from the stamp on the package.

Each South American producer—the people or family who oversaw the cooking of the coca into a paste and then into cocaine—had a unique way to sign or mark their pack-ages so people knew who cooked it. I was fascinated with how much pride the South Americans associated with their product and their reputation, especially given that they might only survive several years. Cooking thousands of kilos of coca leaves into a paste and then into cocaine is dangerous. Literally, the process eats them up, burning their skin, their lungs, their eyes. But they make so much money, more than they could doing anything else in Peru, Bolivia, Colombia, so their families are well taken care of for the rest of their lives.

Seeing this new signature on the kilos worried me until I tested the product for purity. It was just as pure as the cocaine I'd been receiving in Miami after vacation. Then I tested it by snorting a line. The buzz kicked in within a few minutes. Definitely the good stuff.

This small delivery was definitely scaled back from when I'd lived in Miami, when I'd been moving thirty kilos a month and had broken bread with Pablo Escobar. But I was back in business. For every kilo I sold, I made about $15,000. Not bad—$45,000 for a month of work. And, oh man, did I miss that Colombian cocaine. With that first delivery, I snorted for five days straight.

Once the Colombians realized I could still deliver the money from North Carolina, I could get as much as I needed, whenever I needed it. Sometimes, I met Javi at a halfway point, a tavern or barbecue joint or a hotel, usually in Georgia. Other times, he delivered it to me at the auction house. Once, he arrived unannounced; I looked up in the middle of an auction and there he was, grinning and waving at me from the back of the room. I didn't much care for my two worlds overlapping unexpectedly. I jumped off the stage and directed one of the teenaged employees to keep items queued up on the stage for Marvin to sell off. Hustling to the back, I made eye contact with Javi and ticked my head in the direction of my office.

Scooting him inside, I said, "Javi, my man. Que pasa?"

"I got three kilos, in case you need some. Figured you're ready for more."

"Appreciate you thinkin' of me, but I didn't call for any. Hope you didn't come all the way up here just to see me, cuz I don't have the money right now."

He flicked his hand at me. "It's okay. You pay me on my next trip here. You're good for it."

That was an honor, that Gustavo's family and his Miami distributors knew they could rely on me. They knew I could move the cocaine and pay in full, even though I was now a ten-hour drive from Miami. As long as I kept nurturing that connection, I could get whatever quantity I could move.

He went to his car and sauntered right back in with three kilos packed into an Amway cleaning-products box.

"Alright. The Amway Man is here." I always called him Amway Man after that.

The auction barn was the perfect cover for smuggling and provided a great place to stash cocaine. My office had a drop ceiling, with removable ceiling panels. I stood on my desk, pushed one of the panels up and slid the cocaine on top of the three adjacent panels to distribute the weight. Didn't want a ceiling panel crashing down on my desk. I knew exactly which panel I always hid my stash above: when entering my office, it was the eighth panel to the left, third one from the wall. And the stage, from where Marvin auctioned items, had a panel I could remove to stash larger quantities. Of course, that had to be done when the building was empty. At one point, I hid fifteen kilos under the stage. During an auction. Four hundred people in that auction barn looking up at Marvin on the stage, and not a soul knew what was right there in front of them.

Snorted a bunch of cocaine in that auction barn. Often with Rick and Lynn.

Lynn often came down on weekends and worked the concession stand in the back of the auction house for me. I had an inkling that things weren't great in her life when she told me she was taking a break from college. That didn't seem like a good idea to me, because she was always so smart. Plus, Linda had all the tuition money from that back child support. But Lynn wasn't asking my opinion, and I was in no position to give career advice.

Or relationship advice. She was with some doctor or shrink, headed to Hawaii with him. Sounded like he was a lot older than her, but what could I say? At least this guy didn't sound like the type who carried around a sawed-off shotgun.

Pushing her out of my life again didn't make sense if she wanted to be in it. The justification that kept my guilt at bay went like this: if my daughter was using drugs already, at least I could keep her from scrounging around with low-life drug dealers. As a cop, I'd seen first-hand how women in the drug world were treated, used and abused, some-times killed. But she'd be using the best cocaine in the world. What father wouldn't want that? I mean, what father who was a smuggler wouldn't want that? With a daughter who was already using drugs? It was obvious to me that Lynn had already become, without any influence from me, much more than a recreational drug user. Thankfully, unlike Rick, she wasn't working for me. And I planned to keep it that way.

The whole situation was more comfortable when we snorted together. Everything was more comfortable when I was high. And when Lynn visited me, we were always high.

CHAPTER 25
DARK-HAIRED BEAUTY

My world got spun around, crazier than it had ever been, when I laid eyes on this sexy, svelte woman wearing a black beret with thick auburn hair spilling out from underneath it.

She strolled into the auction barn and was the prettiest thing I'd ever seen at one of our auctions. Hell, she was the prettiest thing I'd seen in years. My tryst had ended with the saddlebag-carrying local gal, who never got used to lavish attention or filet mignon. I was getting worried about how slim the pickings were in that small town—and I'm not talking about purses. But that dark-haired beauty gave me a little jolt of hope (and a bigger jolt right between my legs). She was with a much older man, so I figured she was either a hooker or a gold-digger.

I asked my teenaged grunt if he knew who she was, and he scanned the room for the beret I'd described. "Oh, that's Miss Warren. She's a teacher over at the high school."

"A teacher?" Maybe that's her real daddy, not a sugar daddy, I thought. Promising, very promising. But a teacher?

She'd be pretty straitlaced, and I wanted someone I could be myself around. Suzy had spoiled me in that way.

After the auction ended, I made my way over to Miss Warren and introduced myself as one of the owners. She told me her name was Katherine and introduced me to her father (phew!). Her father wandered off—smart man—and she took me in for few seconds, then smiled. "I grew up here, so I know you're not a local. Where're you from?" Oh I loved that Southern accent.

"Well, I wanted to be here near my folks so came up from Miami last year after semi-retiring and—"

"Hold it right there." She held her hand up in front of her, palm facing me, really close to my face. "Semi-retired? At your age? What are you, forty?"

"Yes, ma'am. Forty-four."

"From Miami? If you're involved with drugs, I don't want any part of this."

Gorgeous and damn sharp too. That should've been a signal for me to turn around and walk away. Or to start lying. Instead, I said, "Wait a minute. Slow down there. Why don't you have dinner with me, lemme explain my situation to you? At least get to know me a little before you decide to end it."

She cocked an eyebrow up and stared at me for several long seconds. "Decide to end what?"

"The conversation. Our conversation. Let's at least talk. Over dinner."

To my surprise, she said, "One dinner. But I'm not giving you my address. I'll meet you at the restaurant."

During dinner, I told her about my history—well, most of it. I told her about my three children, my two divorces, my career as a cop, my imprisonment and when my parole would end. I was truly reformed, I assured her.

My parole would end on time, no doubt. Lloyd had never piss-tested me, not once, even when I became brazen around him. Once I snorted a line in the parking lot before going in to see him, then kept my sunglasses on inside his office to hide my dilated pupils. It seemed like he didn't want to arrest me, I don't know why. I think he wanted to go into the auction business when he retired and figured I'd be a good contact.

Anyways, I assured Katherine all of these parts of my life were in the past.

As she listened without saying a word, I was thinking: this is one of the smartest women I've ever met, and I believe I've actually pulled this one off.

In a way, I believed everything I was saying. All of that bad shit *could* be in my past. If I stopped calling Miami, the smuggling would be over. All I needed to do was flip that switch. If we continued to date and got serious. I'd stop smuggling.

Now Katherine wasn't messing around. She was thirty-seven, looking for a committed relationship and wasn't jumping in the sack without one. I pulled out all the stops: romancing her, making her laugh, showering her with attention, gifts, cards, flowers, even wooed her mama, who adored me right away.

Three months later, we were married. Had to be a short engagement, with her holding out for a permanent commit-ment. Two weeks before our wedding, Amway Man deliv-ered several kilos to me, Mike and Rick came down and picked up a few and Bill—who wasn't helping me buy or sell real estate anymore, just cocaine—distributed the rest in Charlotte.

Loaded with cash, we had a no-expenses-spared wedding ceremony and reception, an almost all-night (for me and a few others who were snorting) post-reception party and an amazing honeymoon at Lake Tahoe. We stayed in the nicest resorts, which was good because we spent lots of time in those rooms.

Katherine loved to laugh, and I loved making her laugh. We had a blast on that trip, dining at all the high-end restaurants and wandering through all the boutique shops. I dropped a few thousand dollars to ship home a massive chair made of thickly lacquered, gnarled redwood roots with wide redwood slabs for armrests. The cushions were made of the softest leather. Also bought a matching glass coffee table, which was supported with the same tangled redwood as the chair.

Everywhere we went, every chance I could, I snuck into a restroom, our rental car or a secluded area and snorted a pinch of cocaine.

Shortly after we married, Katherine and I purchased a condo a few units down from one I'd recently purchased for my folks (they were too old to take care of a lawn and a house, and I was too busy smuggling to help them). Once again, my plan was to settle down and enjoy life. I had this nice condo, a beautiful, smart wife, plenty of cash. The time was perfect to quit smuggling.

But Miami kept calling, Amway Man kept bringing me product, Rick, Mike and Bill kept asking for more and I kept pulling the wool over Katherine's eyes.

Getting married slowed me down but didn't stop me. I

didn't think anything could stop me. At first, I didn't bring any coke home, just drank scotch there, especially when I needed to come down from a day of snorting at the auction barn or making a coke run.

By then, I was snorting massive amounts—multiple grams per day. So much that I should've been dead. Running back to the auction barn in the evening when the last line wore off was getting suspicious. How many times could I have forgotten to lock the loading-bay door or turn off the hot-dog machine or turn the heat down or turn off the lights?

Then, lucky for me, Rick and Vanessa moved down that fall to live near me, or at least near their supply. Having them in the same town would be the perfect cover for me. I planned to keep a stash at Rick's place and zip over for a quick snort, otherwise known to Katherine as stopping by to see my son and daughter-in-law.

That great idea quickly proved to be a bad one. Vanessa found out she was pregnant so quit using drugs but Rick didn't stop. My stash became his stash. He smoked anything I left at his house. So, I started asking Rick to run over to the auction barn and grab some blow, so he and I could do a few lines out in his car or out back. This way, we both got a snort, and I regulated his use. At least his crack use.

Rick also worked some auctions for me, partly for the cash and partly, I'm sure, for the coke. If he stopped there— snorting off and on—he might have been able to handle the cocaine and dealing it, but he just couldn't put down that cursed crack pipe. Once he picked that pipe up, he didn't put it down until the coke was gone.

After Katherine went to sleep one night, I called Rick. "You up to makin' a run for me, over to the auction house?"

"It's the middle of the night. Isn't Katherine there?"

"She's out like a light."

"Why don't *you* go then?"

"Don't want her to wake up and find me gone. Come on. It'll give us a chance to chat out in your car."

The phone was silent for several seconds, then he let out a big sigh. "I can't keep doing this, Pop. Nessa and I are about to have a baby. I gotta stay away from the blow."

"Just leave your pipe at home. That's your problem."

"No, the coke's the problem. It's too much for me. Living like this is gonna make you crazy, and it's killin' me. Sorry, but I can't help you this time."

I heard a click and the hum of the dead phone line.

Good for him, I thought. Bad for me though.

My brain moved right on to scheming how to sneak out and get some of that coke. Then I told myself, No, no, no! You can do this. You can stay away from that blow for one night.

I went into the kitchen and poured myself a triple scotch with a splash of water, then planted myself in the living-room chair and turned on the TV with the volume down low, so I wouldn't wake Katherine. I forced myself to stay in that chair, flipping through the channels, looking for anything to occupy my brain, which was screaming for more cocaine. Sipping my scotch, I kept my ass in that chair until I came down from the last line I'd snorted.

After that brutal night, I just started bringing a stash home with me. Found a little spice container that held twenty-eight grams. Now, I didn't pack it full, because I didn't want it spilling all over when I snapped the lid open. If I put around twenty grams in there, that covered my needs for a few days. That wasn't perfect either, because when Katherine was home, I could only go sniffing and snuffing in the bathroom so many times each day. And if I wanted to go for a walk, she'd go with me.

I was a pro at living two lives, which helped me hide my cocaine use and smuggling from Katherine. But I was sick and tired of living a double life after twenty years of doing that. And trying to snort massive amounts of coke without your wife—who is a high-school teacher—finding out wasn't easy. And I was really letting my guard down, which was never good when you're living two lives.

Anytime I was straight, I thought about getting out of the smuggling business. But man, I loved the money. Where could I find a decent job making even one-fourth of my current income? The auction business wasn't as lucrative as I'd hoped, and I hated the idea of selling cars again or some dirtbag job like that.

Like any high-paying job, you get stuck because the money's so good. Even if you hate the job or your boss or your co-workers, you can't walk away from the money. You keep telling yourself you'll quit after the next paycheck. The next month rolls around, and you've got bills to pay, things you want to buy, so you promise yourself you'll quit next month. Before you know it, you're an old man, and all you have to show for your life, if you're lucky, is a decent retirement pension.

No pension plan for smugglers, but I wasn't exactly thinking about the future. I doubted I'd live to be an old man. *Now* was all that mattered, and right *now* I wanted to keep the money coming. I was never ahead as much as I wanted to be. Just one more suitcase of cash. One more kilo. One more line of cocaine.

Every time I made a successful hand-to-hand transaction, I felt like a million bucks and could maintain the delusion I was in control of my world. Moving product from Florida all the way up to Ohio, and who knows where else my stuff ended up, right under the noses of parole officers and law enforcement and DEA and neighbors and Katherine. That required some stealth. Clearly, I was still able to move like the wind in the dark, still invisible. And invincible. I was proud of my relationships with the Colombians, who dominated cocaine trafficking into the U.S. by then. Hell, in the world. Being part of that made me feel powerful. I was addicted to that.

CHAPTER 26
THE TRUTH

Most of the time, I tried treating Katherine like a princess. I could be great at that. For a while. I encouraged her to quit her job, took her shopping, treated her to fancy dinners, made her laugh until she about peed her pants. Her mother was a hoot, and I loved to crack her up too. She was soft-spoken but, like Katherine, wasn't afraid to speak her mind either.

But I couldn't treat Katherine like a princess and be a good smuggler. That princess treatment would end abruptly when, without warning, I'd get aloof and disappear for a day or two to pick up or distribute a shipment. I told Katherine I was buying antiques, but after returning empty-handed a couple of times, she knew something was up. But when she asked, I always denied it.

I came back after one of these two-day disappearances driving a new sports car for Katherine. She was livid. "Where have you been? Don't you dare tell me you went hunting for antiques! And where'd the money come from for this car?"

"I went down to Florida. Sold a house I still owned down there." I walked into the kitchen and poured myself a drink. She followed me.

"How come you never mentioned this house before? Tell me where the money came from, or I'm walking out that door." She pointed at the front door. That would become a familiar gesture of hers in the coming year.

I stared at her with a look on my face that I imagine was about as blank as I felt. My walls went up, way up. Stonewalling was my go-to response when someone boxed me in or, in this case, called me on my bullshit.

"You disappear for *two days* and come back with a flashy car? For me? I don't want that car. I don't want any of this stuff." She rotated around, looking at some of the very expensive antiques I bought her recently. Her voice was growing louder. "I can't take it anymore. Just tell me the truth."

Something had to give, and it wasn't going to be her. Truly, I didn't want her to walk out that door. "Okay. Some-body owed me some money. When I got paid, I wanted to spend it on somethin' special for you."

"Money someone owed you? For drugs?"

"Yeah, but hear me out. I made this deal before I ever met you. The guy finally had the money to pay me back. It's my money, fair and square."

"Fair and square," she yelled. "What part of drug dealing is fair and square? You mean me to believe you're getting money from these people but not selling anymore? That you're not using drugs too? I am *not* going to live with a drug dealer."

Didn't seem important to point out that I was not a

dealer, never was. Those people ran around and sold drugs on the streets. I moved kilos, multiple kilos, to distributors.

She slumped down at the kitchen table. I tried to rub her back, and she shrugged my hand away.

I sat down across from her. "Listen to me. I am *not* smuggling anymore. This is drug money that was owed to me."

She looked at me for several long moments. "Are you telling the truth? Because our marriage depends on it."

I'd lied about so many things in my life. Had lied to save my life, to save Carl's life. Lied to save both my marriages. Lied to end my first marriage. Lied to get a woman. Lied to get rid of a woman. Lied to drug dealers. Lied to police. Lied to buy and sell drugs, on both sides. What was one more? Keeping her was as good a reason as any to lie.

"I swear. It's the truth. If you want me to take the car back, just say the word. In fact, I'll give the damn money back if you want. You're all that matters to me." I reached over and wrapped my hands around hers. She didn't jerk them away.

The anger in her eyes, all over her face, was replaced with resignation, or at least exhaustion. Somehow this intelligent woman was actually going to buy my story. I think she knew, she just didn't want to walk away from me. At least, not yet.

"Get rid of it then. The car and the money. Don't bring any more drug money into this house. Ever."

I sold the sports car later that week and was on my best behavior, which meant I was extra careful, for weeks. Even started going to church with her.

How ironic that I could be smuggling drugs, lying to my wife, snorting cocaine with my own children and somehow feel perfectly at home in church. Church was so familiar and even comforting: the rituals, the hymns, the cadence— even more than the words—of the preacher's sermon, the smell of candles and flowers and women's perfume mingling together, yucking it up with folks afterwards over coffee and donuts. My father always said I'd have been a good preacher.

The reprieve from fighting with Katherine didn't last long. We returned home from church one afternoon, and I turned on the television and dropped into our sofa. As I did, my stash container rattled onto the floor.

"What's that, honey? Looks like a tiny compact. You wearing make-up these days?"

I snatched my container up. "Nothin'."

"What do you mean, nothing? Let me see it." She held out her hand.

I stared at the television. "I said, it's nothing."

"That's full of drugs, isn't it?"

"Just forget about it, alright?"

"No. I won't forget about anything. Two and two has not been adding up to four lately. Again. And drugs would explain a lot of your behavior lately."

"Yeah, it's a little coke, but not mine. Rick asked me to hold on to this for him. He's really strung out on this stuff and wanted it outta his house yesterday."

"Why didn't you flush the drugs down the toilet?"

"Darlin', cocaine isn't cheap. I need to wait and see what he wants me to do with *his* stuff. Maybe he'll—"

"I am *done*." She stood and slipped her shoes back on. "If you want to continue living that life, go right ahead. But your lying is tearing us apart." The front door slammed behind her.

Katherine stayed with her mama for a week, refusing my calls and visits. On the following Sunday, she returned, unannounced. Luckily, I hadn't started snorting and drinking for the day yet.

I'd really missed her company and enveloped her in a big, long hug. "I'm so glad you're back. I missed you so much, just wanderin' around this empty condo." All of this was true.

"Mama told me I was more miserable there at her house without you than I was here at home with you. She told me to go on home and work things out. She's right. I *don't* want to live without you. I really don't. But you have to give up these drugs. I can't live with a drug dealer. Please."

"I'll stop. I swear." And I meant it. I wanted to be done.

For the next few weeks, I stayed away from my stash at the auction barn. I may even have given it to Rick that time, and luckily, I didn't get any calls or visitors from Miami. I romanced Katherine, told her how beautiful she was, made her breakfast every morning and took her out for dinner every evening. I'd never treated her better.

Then one morning, as we were lounging around in bed still, the phone rang. It was Amway Man. I sat up in bed, and that switch was already flipped. I talked into the phone briefly. I'm sure my cryptic conversation didn't make any sense to Katherine, which probably scared the shit out of her and rightly so.

Without so much as a fleeting thought, I hung up and said, "That was Marv. Got some antiques he wants me to go check out. I'll be back late tonight, maybe tomorrow."

She watched me pull my pants on, a stunned look on her face.

She followed me to the bathroom. "*Please* don't do this." Her arms hung at her sides, helpless, no fight left in her.

I preferred her bitching at me with arms crossed angrily across her chest. I ran a comb through my hair and my mustache, avoiding her face in the mirror.

"You can't keep living this way. We don't need the money. I'll go back to work."

I swished mouthwash around in my mouth until my cheeks burned, then spit it into the sink. My hands resting on the counter top, I stared into the sink. "It's not about the money. Well, partly it is … it's just … something I gotta do."

"If you value this marriage, you won't do this."

"I *do* love you. Truly. But if you can't handle this, you do whatever you have to do."

Partway down the stairwell, she grabbed the back of my shirt. "John! Please don't do this."

I hated this. She was a strong woman and seeing her like that made me feel like a son of a bitch. She was the only woman in years who'd seen the real me—at least the small, real parts I let her see through all my lies and scams. The last woman who'd seen much of my true self was Linda, decades earlier. With Laura, I'd been in the clutches of drugs and booze and the promise of easy money, crossing that line from cop to smuggler. I don't know what the hell

Laura saw in me; I must've been a whole lot better at deception then. And Suzy, she saw the real me who was a smuggler: acting cavalier and dripping in money and drugs and fun. But when you're snorting massive amounts of drugs together, you don't really get to know each other.

I don't know why I was doing this, trying to live a double life again. I knew better. A marriage couldn't survive this shit. This was worse than trying to have a family as an undercover agent. But I didn't want to walk away from Katherine either.

But those walls were up already. I was on automatic pilot now.

"It's just work, that's all. I'll be back. I'll always be back. But if you wanna stay married to me, you gotta deal with my work." It was frightening how easily I flipped that switch and walked right out our front door.

So much for being like the wind at night, more like a hurricane in the middle of the day. Not just with Katherine, I was messing up my kids too.

CHAPTER 27
NO TOMORROW

Vanessa gave birth to Dannie, two months premature, that December. He was so tiny. His skin was almost translucent. Made me queasy to see my grandson in that plastic hospital warmer, tubes all over him. Rick was tearful, pacing helplessly between Vanessa's room and the neonatal ICU. Watching that tiny newborn fight for his life scared us all.

But that little guy was a fighter, grew stronger every day.

Shortly after the doctors let them take Dannie home from the hospital, Rick made a coke run for me up to Mike in Ohio. He drove up, made the exchange and drove straight back.

When he met me at the auction house with my money, he'd obviously snorted the whole way up and back. His pupils were dilated, he was talking a mile a minute, sweaty and clammy looking, chain-smoking.

He dropped the briefcase on my desk. "Here's your money. But that's the last job I do for you. If I keep this up, next thing you know I'll be drivin' down to Miami and up to Ohio for you every month. One pinch of that shit sets me off, and I can't stop.

"You wanna be a father to me or a grandpa to Dannie, fine. But don't ever ask me to do anything"—he held his hands up in front him, surrendering—"with coke again. Never. I'm out."

I think he was really done this time. Thank goodness for both of us—him for obvious reasons, and me because who needs to deal with all that guilt.

Lynn came down to meet Dannie that spring. After she visited Rick and Vanessa, we spent our usual weekend at the auction: me scuttling antiques up to the stage for Marvin to sell, Lynn working the concession stand and, in between, us snorting line after line in my office. Every time I headed back to my office for a pinch of that nose candy, like clock-work, she'd be rapping on my door a few minutes later.

Me and Lynn were in and out of my office all evening. That auction barn was packed full of people, hundreds of them, no one even noticed she and I ducking in and out of my office all night long. I remember getting into my ceiling panel to replenish my stash container before we went home. That means we'd snorted several grams between the two of us.

By the end of the night, we were blitzed. Then we had to go home and face Katherine. I hated to put Lynn through that: facing her new step-mom after snorting blow all day. If we were lucky, Katherine would be asleep.

She was dozing on the couch, doing what any good stepmother would do, waiting up to see her new step-daughter. That's some bad shit, having to act straight around someone—especially your wife, can't imagine your stepmother—when it feels like people are watching your every move and all you want to do is hide or snort another line.

Katherine walked up and gave Lynn a big bear hug. "It's so good to see you." Then she held her at arm's length. "How are you?"

Poor Lynn, I thought. But she forced a smile and looked Katherine right in the eyes. Oh, she was good; really took after her old man.

"I'm great," Lynn said. "Little tired. Dad worked me hard at the auction barn. How are you?"

Katherine swatted at me. "Honey, did you make her work all night?"

"Yep. No free rides here," I said, clicking my tongue. While they chatted, I got myself a scotch and took a big swallow. Standing behind Katherine, I wiggled my scotch glass at Lynn and raised my eyebrows in question.

She shook her head.

Well, that was my best offer—scotch. Next best thing I could do was get her up to the guest bedroom. But all things considered, all our lines of cocaine considered, Lynn was acting pretty cool.

"Well, let the girl hit the sack, darlin'," I said to Katherine. "Told you, she worked her butt off at the auction." I carried Lynn's suitcase to the bottom of the stairs, trying to keep things moving in the right direction.

"Wait. I have something for her." Katherine walked to the living room, motioning for us to follow. Lynn looked trapped and miserable. I shrugged, and we followed Katherine.

Lynn glanced around the living room. "Wow, where'd you guys get this new furniture?"

"That's right, you haven't been here since our wedding. Your daddy got that on our honeymoon. In Lake Tahoe."

"They cost as much to ship as I paid for 'em. Solid redwood. Just love 'em. Try the chair." The leather cushions exhaled when she sunk into them. "Gotta a little gas there?" I chuckled, trying to lighten things up. Lynn rolled her eyes at me.

Katherine, grinning, handed Lynn a wrapped package.

She fidgeted with it. "Should I open it now?"

"Go ahead. We ain't got all night," I said. I unfurled a roll of antacids, popped two in my mouth and held the roll up to Lynn. She looked at me quizzically, shook her head. Guess she didn't inherit ulcers from me. Not yet.

Lynn opened the gift: an enlarged photo from our wedding. "Oh, I love it. Thank you so much." She turned it around so we could all see it: me and Katherine in a tux and wedding gown, Lynn on one side and my mother on the other. By the time that picture had been taken, I was snorting and drinking up a storm. So was Lynn, if I recalled correctly. From the look of her eyes in that photo, dark and dilated, my recall was spot-on. In the photo, we both had smiles pasted on our faces, like we did right now sitting in the living room. The mask of the wired: dark, glassy eyes, flushed cheeks, fake grins.

"Well, honey," Katherine said, "I wanted you to have this to remember what an important part of our lives you are."

Mask on. I forced a smile and nodded in agreement. "Now can you let this poor thing get to bed?"

"Yeah, I'm wiped out," Lynn said. "I'll see you guys in the morning."

"We're so glad you're here," Katherine said, standing and giving her another hug.

I nudged Lynn towards the stairs. "C'mon. I'll take your suitcase on up for you."

After I put her suitcase in the guest bedroom, I asked if she needed anything else, palming my stash container at her.

To my surprise, she shook her head and whispered, "No way. I have to get some sleep, so I can face her"—she tipped her head towards me and Katherine's bedroom—"in the morning."

I shrugged and slid it back in my pocket. "Suit yourself. Goodnight, darlin'. Love you."

As I climbed into bed with Katherine, I was out of sorts. Seeing that photo of myself and my daughter, wired on coke at my wedding and wired again tonight around Katherine. All hard evidence: I was a lousy father and husband.

Since Rick swore off the cocaine, I hadn't seen him for a while. After Lynn's visit to meet Dannie and our blitz in the auction barn, I hadn't heard from her for a couple of months either. I assumed she stopped using cocaine or was trying to. Everything in my life was moving fast and wild: drugs, money, Amway Man, Mike, Bill. So when Rick and

Lynn stopped coming around, I figured it was just as well they didn't get caught up in all that anymore.

It wasn't that I didn't want to see them, it's just that I was in no condition to even pretend to be a dad. Working with Rick and using with Lynn had been eating away at me, even though I kept plowing right on through any flashes of my conscience telling me doing this with my kids was wrong. So, when they stopped coming around, I didn't have to try to refrain from using with them or limit Rick's access or, heaven forbid, talk about what'd been going on between us.

My kids seemed to have done what I couldn't do: walked away from the drugs. And to do that, suppose they had to walk away from me.

The other thing that happened was that all my sneaking and lying and arguing with Katherine was sucking the excitement out of smuggling. She didn't understand, or wouldn't admit to herself, exactly what was happening, but on some level, she must've known. On top of that, my lack of sleep and the physical wear and tear on my forty-five-year-old body was catching up with me.

I was still connected with the South Americans, putting deals together in North Carolina and Ohio, but I wasn't distributing much anymore. In my heyday, I moved thirty kilos a month, then I bought and sold a few kilos every month.

Visits and calls from Miami dwindled as I took longer and longer to move each shipment. After I finished each load, I told myself it was my last one. But after I paid for each shipment, including any of the coke I snorted or kept for later, I never had as much money as I planned. I could've made a lot more money if I hadn't been snorting, but with access to so much, I never thought about things like that. I wasn't exactly doing any accounting—of money or blow.

Sometimes I got a delivery from Amway Man and thought, God, I wish I didn't have to deal with this shit. In such small quantities, and, given my waning interest, I was losing track of my lies, my stash, my double lives. Sometimes I wondered if a half-kilo that I forgot about was still stashed away somewhere.

Unfortunately, my interest in snorting hadn't waned in the slightest. I used so much coke during that first year of my marriage, I should've been dead. That's some crazy shit. Since Katherine wasn't working anymore, I seldom snorted at home. Nothing kills a buzz like having to act straight around someone who's not using with you. So, mostly I got high in my office during the day.

One day, mid-week, Marvin was out of town buying some antiques, so I was free to use coke all day in there without having to hide anything. My tolerance for cocaine had skyrocketed by then, and I didn't even bother keeping track of how much I was using. Didn't need to. I had plenty.

By evening, I'd snorted so much, I was wired out of my mind. Then I got to thinking what I'd do if Lloyd showed up. I couldn't pull the wool over his eyes. If he saw me in this condition, I'd get piss-tested. And if I got tested, I'd go back to prison. Once my mind latched onto that thought, it started spiraling out of control.

Realizing how much I'd let my guard down since moving out of Miami, I was certain I was being watched.

Thinking of every surveillance technique I knew of, I began scouring the building. Carrying a screwdriver around, I checked under and inside every object in my office where a mic could be concealed. Good thing we weren't full of antiques that day—would've been lots of drawers to check and lamps to take apart. I fingered every hole, stuffed wadded-up newspaper in holes I couldn't fit my finger in, ran my hand along every dusty ledge and under every counter.

Each action would relieve my anxiety for a while, then I'd go back to the office, snort another line, kick back and enjoy the bliss, then twenty, thirty minutes later, my paranoia would explode again.

I scurried around locking all the windows, dragging a stepladder with me to lock the high ones that we never bothered to latch. None of this relieved my growing fear, so I slid open the door of the loading bay, dashed out to my car and drove it inside the building. If Lloyd came by and didn't see my car outside, he'd just drive on by. By then I was panting and my shirt was stuck to my back with sweat.

As I was sliding my desk so it wasn't visible from the window—I'd closed the blinds earlier but was afraid Lloyd could see through the slats—when I heard wheels rolling into the gravel parking lot. I peeked through the blinds and, sure as shit, it was Lloyd.

Dropping to my knees, I crawled under my desk and took long, slow breaths. I was sure I'd have a heart attack right then and there. That's how it was all going to end. They'll find me, dead, hunkered under my desk like a coward.

Lloyd knocked on the front door once, then again

louder. BAM! BAM! BAM! My arms and legs were blazing with adrenaline, which did me no good because I wasn't running anywhere. The knocking stopped. My bad knee, which was folded underneath me, was screaming in pain, so I rolled onto my side and stretched that leg out, keeping as much of my upper body wedged under the desk as possible. Only time in my life I wished I wasn't six feet tall.

Holding my breath, I listened for any sounds from outside. Only my heartbeat pounding in my ears. Then, BAM! BAM! on the back bay doors. *God, let him leave. I swear, I won't do this anymore.* The knocking stopped, and I began breathing again.

A moment later, I heard footsteps in the gravel right outside my window. I broke out in a cold sweat. There was no way he could see me, but I pulled my leg back under my desk, just in case. Then silence again. Something settled out in the auction house, releasing a small squeak that echoed off the metal ceiling.

Then, miraculously, Lloyd's car started up. And those wheels rolled back out of the gravel lot.

My shirt was drenched in sweat, and my body and brain were spent. I flopped onto my back, legs stretched out to get the blood flowing to my feet again. I stared at the bottom of the desk drawer for several minutes, until my pulse finally slowed down.

I'd seen firsthand how things could end for drug smugglers, seen it from both sides. That incident got me thinking that I'd been smuggling for several years—minus that vacation in the middle. That's a pretty damn good run for a smuggler. After hiding under my desk waiting for my heart to explode, I understood that I was pushing the envelope on my good run. It got me thinking that I should stop while I was still a free man. While I was still alive. I was snorting and smuggling coke like there was no tomorrow, but there was a time in the near future when I wouldn't have another tomorrow.

CHAPTER 28
BURNING

didn't call Miami, or respond to any calls, for two months. Those were good months for me and Katherine. When I went that long without disappearing, I imagine she hoped I was truly done. We went to her mama's house for a Fourth of July dinner: barbecued spare ribs, fresh corn on the cob, coleslaw, cornbread and apple pie. That was the best Southern meal around, and all of it homemade. Man, could her mama cook. Their family barbecue-sauce recipe was sweet and spicy with so much vinegar, just a sniff would clear your sinuses. Loved that stuff. Katherine always gave me an extra bowl on the side for dipping. Her mama baked cornbread in a preheated iron pan coated with bacon grease, so the bottom crust was crunchy and a little salty.

As they cooked, my mouth was salivating, but my stomach was burning. My gut had been hurting bad for weeks. Nothing would soothe it. Before sitting down at the table, I dumped a heaping spoon of baking soda into a small glass of water and drank it.

Katherine watched me pick at my meal and said, "Honey, are you feeling alright? I have *never* seen you eat less than a plate of Mama's ribs."

"My stomach's really botherin' me lately. Feels like it's on fire. Nothin' takes the burning away. I can hardly eat anything."

"I keep telling you, you've got to see a doctor. Just go on in and see my doctor."

"Think I will. This is the worst my ulcers have ever been."

After an initial appointment, and a follow-up procedure where they looked into my esophagus and stomach with an endoscope, the doctor recommended surgery. "John, those are some of the worst ulcers I've seen. There's not much holding your esophagus to your stomach. That area there has multiple ulcers and some tearing. Let me ask you"—he looked at me, his face serious and frowning—"do you drink a lot of alcohol?"

"Not sure what you consider a lot. I enjoy a good scotch in the evenings."

"It's common with alcoholics—"

"I'm not an alcoholic."

"It's just an area, right there where the esophagus empties into the stomach, where ulcers occur in, let's just say, in heavy drinkers."

When I was younger, on the police force, I drank heavily, sure, but I didn't consider myself a heavy drinker anymore. A frequent drinker, but not a heavy one. I shook my head. "Nope. Not a heavy drinker either."

"Hmm. It's probably from your long-standing acid reflux. Regardless, you'll need surgery. And soon. But for now, and after your surgery, it's best you avoid the scotch. And any alcohol."

While he handed me papers to read about pre-surgery diet and described the surgery and post-op recovery, my brain was churning about how long it had been since my last deal and how much money I needed for the surgery. There's no insurance in the smuggling line of work. And if I went too long before I purchased more product or delivered some to my distributors, I could be out.

That line of work requires you to stay in the game and stay in touch. Once you lose touch, you don't have a sense of what's going on, who's doing what with who, who's getting sloppy or risky. Losing your connections is how you lose control.

And when connections don't hear from you for a long while, they get suspicious when you suddenly pop back up. They wonder if you've been sitting in jail somewhere, if you're now an informant.

Despite the smuggling losing its appeal, the thought of losing my connections was out of the question. I was proud that I'd maintained the trust of the Colombians for so long. That was rare, and I didn't want to let them down.

"How long after surgery before I can go back to work?"

He glanced at my chart. "You lift the antiques?"

"Yeah, but I can get my young guys to do that."

"We'll keep you in the hospital for a day, maybe two, until you're able to eat solids. Then if you follow all the post-op instructions, eat soft, low-acid foods, low-fat"—he pointed at the papers he'd handed me—"you should be fine to start work again within a week. You'll have to take it easy—no lifting or pushing heavy objects around."

My surgery was scheduled for nine days later. I called Nico and put a deal together right away. Mike was willing to drive down from Ohio for two kilos, Bill wanted one kilo if he could pay me $30,000 now and $10,000 in a few weeks. He was good for it.

Amway Man couldn't drive the load all the way up to me, so I met him at a halfway point in Georgia. As soon as I got back with the product, the first thing I did was a big, fat line. Then I hid a few ounces in my ceiling panels and filled my stash container. All of this I did automatically, without a thought. Then I distributed the rest and deposited the profit in my auction-company bank account.

That was *my* pre-op prep a week before surgery. Definitely not what the doctor ordered.

The day before my surgery, I wasn't to eat anything after ten p.m., which was no problem because everything I ate tore my gut up. I'd been living on scrambled eggs, bananas, ice cream and had even steered clear of scotch. That's how bad my stomach burned. But I was snorting coke like mad.

The morning of my surgery, in the bathroom with the shower running, I snorted the last of my stash. Then I got in the car with Katherine and drove to the hospital.

When I awoke after my surgery, I expected the pain in my gut would finally be gone. The pain was worse. Different, but worse. The doctor explained that once he got in there, the ulceration was extensive, some areas perforated even, so he had to remove portions of my stomach. Basically, he pulled my stomach up and stitched it back onto my esophagus. At least that's what my brain, fuzzy from the anesthesia, understood.

The doctor also said I was lucky, because there was no

sign of infection or gangrene. Hell, I didn't even know a person could get gangrene in their gut. He cautioned me that my recovery would be slow due to the severity of the ulcers and the extent of the surgery.

The next morning, they brought me a special post-surgery meal. As soon as the smell of soft-boiled eggs wafted towards me, I felt a wave of nausea. The first bite made me gag. Over the next few days, my condition worsened. The smell of food, all of it—bland soup, vanilla milkshakes, chocolate pudding—made me retch. Then just the thought of food made me gag. And the stabbing pain in my gut, like I'd been shot through the stomach, was relentless.

They ran tests and drew blood but couldn't find an explanation. Medication only dulled the pain. When they told me they planned to insert a feeding tube through my nose to get food into my body without me having to eat, I agreed. Having a feeding tube inserted didn't sound like a big deal—a thin, flexible tube in my nose—and I didn't care what they did as long as I didn't have to eat anything. The doctor didn't mention he'd be inserting that tube while I was fully conscious.

That was miserable, trying to swallow and stay relaxed while something akin to a snake crawled down my nose and throat.

Rick came in for a visit on day five or six. Since I wasn't expecting to be in the hospital that long, I wanted him to go get my money from Bill. Didn't involve him handling any coke, just money, no big deal. So, when he got ready to leave, I motioned for him to come closer. When he leaned in, I could smell the cigarette smoke on his breath and clothes. Oh God, what I would've done for a cigarette.

"Listen, I got a small pick-up I'm wondering if you could make for me. From Bill. Remember him, my real estate agent? Should be ten grand he still owes me for a kilo I sold him last month. You can meet him at the auction barn, get the—"

"You've gotta be fuckin' kidding me." He stepped back away from the bed. His eyes were wide, his mouth hanging open. "You're layin' here in the hospital ... looks like you're dyin' ... and you want me to go make a deal for you. For what? Ten thousand lousy bucks? What the hell good is that money if you're dead next week? This shit is nuts. I ain't doin' it."

Rick stormed out of the room, shaking his head in disbelief. Or maybe disgust.

Over the next few days, I got worse and started vomiting blood, so they removed the feeding tube. Turns out having a snake crawl out your throat and nose is way easier than having one crawl in. Thank God, they knocked me out before they inserted a scope, also down my nose and throat, so they could see inside my stomach. All they could tell was that the site of the surgery didn't appear to be healing. Still no sign of infection or gangrene. Some kind of good news.

The pain was excruciating, worse than when I'd been shot in the arm. Mostly, I hated being in that hospital. For years my dad was in and out of hospitals. I didn't want my life to end that way for me. If I was dying, I just wanted to go on home and die in peace without all the tubes and needles and meds and doctors and nurses.

Three weeks later, I was lying in bed at another hospital where they transferred me, one with more specialists who were supposed to be able to help me. I was going downhill and fast. Katherine was like a mama bear demanding to know what they were doing to find out what was wrong, what their treatment plan was. I was so grateful, because I was too weak and out of it on pain meds to speak up for myself.

Katherine came into the room one morning to find me curled on my side. She sat next to me, looking helpless.

"Katherine, I gotta see my dad."

"Honey, he can't visit you. They've got him on bedrest again, because his blood pressure's shot up really high."

I tucked my knees closer to my chest, holding my gut. "Then you gotta call him for me. I've gotta talk to him. I don't think I'm gonna make it here."

"I'll call him, but you are not—I repeat—not—going to die."

"I'm so sorry. Sorry I … married you and put you through all this. What a terrible husband I've been."

She turned my face to hers. "You listen to me. I love you. I did not wait until I was thirty-seven to get married just to end up a widow a year later. You are not dying, so stop saying that."

Katherine dialed my dad and handed me the phone.

Hearing his voice, words just poured out of me, don't know why. "Pop, I need you to pray for me. I got a bad feeling I'm not gonna recover from this surgery." I have to admit, I hadn't prayed, or even thought about praying, in a long time. Besides the time I was hiding under my desk from my P.O., but I don't think that kind of prayer counted. My father believed in prayer. And at that moment, I needed to believe in something. Anything.

CHAPTER 29
NO GAME LEFT

A few days later, I was drifting in and out of that fuzzy pain-med sleep, when I heard the door swing open. Rolling my head over to see who it was, Katherine stood by my bed. Her eyes were puffy and red. *This is it. They finally figured out what's wrong. I bet it's cancer. I'm dying. I just know it.* By that point, I wanted any news about what was wrong with me, because I wanted to either get better or go on and die.

As soon as she started talking, I realized she wasn't sad, she was angry.

"I just got off the phone with your daughter. Lynn told me everything. All about your cocaine habit and your smuggling and your lies. And don't you dare try to talk your way out of this. I am *done.*"

Not angry, furious. I waved away her concerns. Just lifting my arm was work. How pathetic to be wasting away in a hospital. I always imagined I'd leave this world in a flash of excitement. "Can we can talk about this when—"

"No! We're talking about it today. With the doctor. When

he comes in here again, if you don't tell him about your drug use, all of it, as much as I hate to do it, I'll walk out that door"—she jabbed her finger in that direction—"and you will *never* see me again."

"What's all this gotta do with my surgery? Doctor won't care about any of that."

"Lynn's worried it might have something to do with your stomach, and now that I know, I am too. You're not getting any better, in case you haven't noticed. Let the doctor decide if it's part of the problem. Maybe the cocaine destroyed your stomach." She glared at me for a minute. "It's your choice: me or the cocaine. You pick."

I nodded and closed my eyes. The whole conversation exhausted me. I couldn't make any sense out of why Lynn told Katherine about my drug use, or why I should tell the doctor. But I had no fight left in me. No scam, no resistance, no lies.

My whole family, what was left of it, was walking away from me. Rick had stormed out. I hadn't seen Lynn in several months. And now Katherine was done with me, or damn close.

When she returned late that afternoon, she got right to the point. "Has the doctor been in yet?"

"I don't know. I've been asleep."

"Good. I want to be here when you tell him everything."

Clearly, she was not letting this go. I could hardly hold my eyes open, but I could tell from her voice she was still pissed. Here I was dying, and everyone was pissed at me.

She dropped a bulky envelope with no return address on the bed next to me. "Marv brought this by. Said it was delivered to you at the auction house. I already opened it."

Bill had delivered my money. Probably heard from Marvin that I was in the hospital and figured I could use the money. Before I could say anything, she dumped the contents on the bed: twenties, fifties and a few hundred-dollar bills. She glared at me, her mouth pursed, daring me to make an excuse.

"It's from an associate," I said. At least I still had some principles. I wasn't telling her our real estate agent was selling cocaine for me. "He owed it to me."

She stuffed the cash back in the package. "I don't want this money. I don't want any of it. Just touching this cash makes me sick."

"Throw it away then. Burn it. Do what you want. I don't care. Should be about ten thousand there."

She looked down at the envelope, then back at me, her lips pressed in a straight line now.

"I really don't care about the money anymore," I said.

"I'll tell you what I'm doing with this money. I'm going straight downstairs and making a payment on your hospital bill." She turned and stomped from the room.

When the doctor came, Katherine dropped down into the chair next to my bed and listened to my latest test results, what the plan was for treatment today, on and on. I wasn't really paying attention anymore. Katherine had none of her usual questions or requests. Stone, cold silent.

As the doctor stood, she turned her face to me with a blank expression. She was gone already.

I put my hand up in front of the doctor. "Wait a minute … before you go … there's something I need to talk to you about."

The doctor sat back down. "Sure. What is it?"

"Well, I doubt this has anything to do with my stomach, but I'm desperate here. Feel like I'm dyin'. So, I thought …" I glanced over at Katherine. "We thought you should know … I have a history of drug use. Cocaine. I've been using it, off and on, for some time now."

The doctor looked back and forth between Katherine and me. "What kind of cocaine use are we talking about here?"

"I've been using it regularly for, oh, about"—I stared at the ceiling, calculating how long it had been since my release from prison—"three years."

"How much? How often?"

"Some months, I use it every day. Some months, maybe two, three weeks outta the month. Sometimes only several days a month. Then sometimes I go for weeks or a month without using any at all."

The doctor stared at me for several moments, then flip open my chart and scribbled. "Are you snorting it?"

I nodded.

"No smoking it or intravenous use?"

I shook my head.

"How much do you use on any given day?"

Now I stared at him. So much cocaine, such large quantities. He wasn't going to believe me. Katherine, if she could even comprehend these quantities, was going to have a shit fit.

"On average?" he added.

I released a big exhale, less to brace myself for this truth-telling and more at the relief of letting it all out finally. "Let's see. On the lower end, two to three grams a day." He raised his eyebrows, then scribbled more in my chart. "At the very high end, I'd say ... close to ten grams a day."

He stopped scribbling. His jaw didn't drop open, but I could tell he was stunned. "Ten grams? John, that amount of cocaine could be lethal."

"Well, I weighed more then. Like two hundred pounds. And I didn't snort it all at once. That would've been over the course of a day. Twenty-four hours, not just a ten- or twelve-hour day. You know, twenty-four hours without sleeping."

"When was the last time you used cocaine?"

I rolled my head over and looked at Katherine. "You sure you wanna hear all this?"

"Oh, I'm sure."

I looked back at the doctor. "The night before I was admitted for surgery."

Katherine let out a groan.

"It's good you told me," the doctor said. "This could be what damaged your esophagus and stomach. You're lucky to be alive." More scribbling. "I need to consult with another doctor, do a little research. But this could help us determine the best treatment plan. I'll talk with the psychiatrist on the chemical-dependency unit too. See what he recommends."

The next day, I was transferred to the drug-treatment unit. By then, I hadn't eaten for over a month. I was gaunt, my cheeks sunken and the skin around my eyes dry and gray. I looked and felt like death was knocking on my door. A shrink came to talk with me. I did my best to explain about the lifestyle and the game, and how I couldn't get enough of it. The doctor listened, nodded occasionally, scribbled notes, asked me to tell him more about this or that.

The thing is, I wasn't much for that kind of talking. Never was. Linda had tried to get me to see a counselor with her before the divorce, but I was this young narcotics agent, full of myself and all that bravado. No Miami undercover agents saw counselors. We were badasses. I still thought of myself as a badass—a badass smuggler. Course I was flat-out on a hospital bed getting all my nourishment through an IV drip. But I still couldn't see how talking about cocaine would help.

What did help was that every evening, the same nurse came on duty after dinner to work the night shift. When she made her rounds, she sat down at the edge of my bed and chatted with me. She wasn't like the psychiatrist, questioning me or trying to understand me. We just talked. Mostly, I talked.

I'm not sure why, but each night I told her a little bit more about my life. Without flinching or even raising an eyebrow, she listened to everything I said. I told her about my early life in Hawaii with Linda and how promising life looked for me then. About how much I loved being a father when my kids were little. Told her about Laura and how I hadn't seen Julie since she was five. I described what it was like being an undercover agent, and how exciting that work was and then how I lost myself and eventually my family. Then I told her all about my smuggling, how I'd lost my second family, prison, smuggling on parole, being forced out of Miami, using coke with my own children. Over the course of a few evenings, I told that nurse everything.

For the first time in years, I felt a huge weight lift off of me, a weight that I didn't even realize I'd been carrying. I felt a lightness, like I was floating in that warm Caribbean Sea.

By the fourth day there, I tried to eat again. They offered me an English muffin, lightly toasted so the edges had a little crunch, but the center was soft and chewy. Butter was pooling in the air pockets. My mouth started watering immediately, but I wasn't gagging. As I held the first bite in my mouth waiting to see if I'd retch, my salivary glands squirted painfully in response to the salty-buttery flavor. Slowly, I began chewing and by the time I'd eaten the first half—and I'm not even ashamed to admit it—tears rolled down my face.

Forget barbecued ribs, escargot and filet mignon; that buttery English muffin was the best food I'd ever tasted. Finally, my stomach didn't tighten or twist in pain or gurgle with acid, it only growled for more. I had to wait an hour before the nurse let me eat anything else. I ordered another English muffin.

It's silly, but that damn English muffin, and the nurse who listened without judgement to all the crap I'd done, got me thinking maybe, just maybe, I'd survive.

As I moved around more, I became aware of how weak I'd become lying around in a hospital bed for over a month. God, I wanted out. Each day I felt a little better. Each day, I wanted nothing more than to go home. The shrink wanted me to stay for the full chemical-dependency program, thirty days, but there wasn't much more I wanted to talk to this guy about. I said all I wanted to say. Once I was able to get in and out of bed by myself, walk down the hall and eat full meals, I was ready to get the hell out of there.

Wouldn't you know, the next thought that came to me was: Wonder when I can get back to work. Thinking about my business, and I don't mean the auction company, was habit. Just like any other job, I guess. I'd been buying and selling product for so many years, thinking about it was automatic. I always thought about my next shipment, how much my distributors needed, how much I'd ask Nico for, calculating how much money I needed and how much money I'd make, where I'd meet Amway Man. And underneath all of the scheming was always my hankering for a big line of that flaky, fish-scale Colombian and the bliss it offered. The bliss that would make me feel like that Thanksgiving gentleman again. Classy and in charge of my world.

Lucky for me, my next thought was the memory of hiding under my desk in the auction barn, waiting to have a heart attack.

When I walked out of that hospital, my gut wasn't burning anymore. But I'd lost my fire for smuggling.

CHAPTER 30
MAYBE NEXT TIME

While I was settling back into life at home and regaining my strength, thoughts of smuggling often popped into my mind. Mostly, I ignored them. When they persisted, I reminded myself what was at stake for me. Katherine was done with all that, and I was done hiding from her. I really cared about her, and, even though I found her under false pretenses, our relationship was still legitimate. I didn't want to lose her. So that left me one option: stay the hell away from the smuggling.

Surprisingly, considering how much I snorted every day, giving up the cocaine was the easier part. As long as I wasn't around any. Now if someone showed up at my door with a big bag of blow, I'd have been hard-pressed not to say, *Well, come on in.* But I'd been down that road so many times, had snorted so much of the *best* cocaine in the world, for so long, that there wasn't anything greater for me to experience by doing more of it. There was no greater high out there than what I'd already experienced.

When I was smuggling, it wasn't unusual for me to go a few days without snorting, like when I needed a clear head in South America or when I had to meet with my P.O. I was capable of restraining myself. So, once I was discharged from the hospital and didn't have any stash, I didn't use. Then, all I had to do was stay away from the cocaine for another day, then another. And the days without snorting slowly added up. When thoughts of cocaine popped into my head, I reminded myself that I chose to have Katherine in my life rather than the drugs. Tried that already. Rode that train as far as I could.

Now, the calls from Miami, they were harder to handle. Whenever one of my connections from Miami called to make a delivery, I kept saying I couldn't help them that month. "Javi, my Amway Man. Sure appreciate you thinkin' of me, but I been in the hospital and haven't moved anything in months. My contacts are scattered around in different places now. Catch me on the next run." I just couldn't burn that bridge. Guess I thought maybe, some-day, if I ever needed or wanted to, I could call them up and make a deal right away. I'd worked so long and hard to build those relationships, I just couldn't bear the thought of losing the Colombians' confidence.

While I never said I was out of the business, eventually the calls stopped. If I'd still lived in Miami, they may have persisted a while longer, but it's a ten-hour drive to North Carolina, and driving dirty is no fun. They had easier connections closer to Miami. They weren't going to drive all the way up for a barbecue.

What did come to mind more frequently than I expected, more frequently than I feared, was the lifestyle I'd left behind. I don't think that I was addicted to cocaine. Yes, I'd developed an extremely high tolerance for it—even for a big man like me, snorting several grams a day is a lot of blow. But the one thing more electrifying than the sight of a few kilos of the finest cocaine in the world, was the sight of a grocery bag or a couple of suitcases full of cash. It was that lifestyle I was addicted to. I craved the intensity and risk, the clandestine handoffs, the scheming and scamming, the huge payoffs, the elation of pulling a job off without getting caught by the DEA or parole officers. And that money, that easy money. I never stopped wanting that.

Where I used to feel euphoria, right in my gut, from that lifestyle, I now felt, sort of, bland. I craved being able to drop five, six hundred bucks at a restaurant if I wanted to splurge on an elaborate meal and drinks. Unable to shower friends and family with extravagant, impulsive gifts was stifling. That was how I always expressed my affection and love. I didn't have anything exciting to offer anyone now; I was dull and boring. Katherine kept saying she'd had all the excitement she needed for one marriage.

Katherine and I were getting along, but underneath was all that old garbage. She probably trusted me as far as she could throw me. I'm sure she was waiting for that switch to flip inside me, for me to walk out the door and disappear for a couple of days.

She insisted that we see a counselor, which I was not overjoyed about, but I figured I owed her that much. On the way to our first counseling session, I was tapping my fingers on the steering wheel, flipping from one radio station to another and dreading what we were about to do.

She was going to be upset with what I had to say, or what I wouldn't say. Either way was a no-win situation for me. If I was truthful about my past, the details would scare the shit out of her. If I lied or held back, she'd accuse me of being dishonest.

When we pulled into the parking lot, I finally spit it out. "Listen, I'm not gonna say much in there. You know how private I am. I'll go, but I may not say a word. You'll have to do all the talkin'."

She shifted in her seat to face me. "Have you ever known that to be a problem for me?" We both cracked up laughing. We hadn't laughed like that in a long time.

One of the first things the counselor said to us was, "Let me ask you two, are you here because your marriage is over or because you want to save it?"

Katherine looked at me then back to the counselor. "Well, my answer depends on his." She pointed her thumb at me.

The counselor looked at me.

"I wanna save the marriage. It's the best thing that ever happened to me. But … I'm not sure I can. Think I've done a little damage."

Katherine's mouth fell open slightly. "Oh, you do, huh? A *little* damage?"

I looked back at the counselor. "Okay. I've done a *lot* of damage."

"What I want is for you to be honest with me," Katherine said. "And to let me in."

"Let you in? Into what? My mind? Trust me darlin', you do *not* want to go there."

"You know what I mean. Let me know who you really are. I've already seen the worst of it. And, in case you haven't noticed, I'm still here. And I don't think that … drug dealer was who you really are."

Honestly, I didn't know who the hell I was anymore. If I wasn't a smuggler, ducking and swirling around everyone in my life, invisible, then who was I? If I went back to who I was before that, I was a police officer. And that man was long gone.

Over time, I saw there were parts of me, the best parts, that were the same as when I was on the force. I still had quite a knack with people, putting them at ease, drawing them out. Maybe I was that way before I became a policeman, and why I was so good at undercover work. And smuggling.

And, I believed in following orders, at least at a societal level. That was a good part of me. You'd never find me beating on or being disrespectful to women. Or protesting at any riots; I'd been to enough of those as a cop. Even as a smuggler, I followed the codes of any respectable smuggler. Followed them all to a T. That's one of the reasons I had such a good, long run.

For better or worse, parts of me were still intact from when I was a smuggler too. Those parts ran pretty deep and were hard to shake. I never fully stopped paying attention to what was happening all around me, what everyone was doing and with who. But that wasn't a bad thing, just tiring. And I didn't need that vigilance anymore in a little town in North Carolina.

I'll never forget the first time I just walked out my front door and went to the grocery store without a second thought. Didn't realize it until the bagger handed me my grocery sack. Got a little zap of awareness that I'd let my guard down, then chuckled to myself. I didn't have anything to hide. I was just a middle-aged man with a sack full of groceries.

It was relaxing not having to watch my back anymore. Any arrests I'd made were long ago and down in Florida. And I never did anything as a smuggler to warrant revenge. Now, I could be an open book with most folks.

Much to my surprise, people still enjoyed my company, even without all the cash and coke. But in the back of my mind, there was always the thought that if so-and-so only knew the truth about me, about my past, they wouldn't be hanging out with me for long. Like Lynn and Rick. They knew the truth about me, and they were keeping their distance.

The first Father's day after my surgery, Katherine asked if I wanted to do something special.

"What for?" I asked.

"To celebrate Father's Day."

"Nah. I got no reason to celebrate that."

"Sure you do. You have three kids. That's a reason. I don't know why you're giving up on having a relationship with them."

"Think I burned that bridge pretty bad. My life was so screwed up for so long, they were better off without me. Probably just as well, would've screwed 'em up worse if I'd been around more."

"But your life *isn't* screwed up anymore."

"Yeah, but they don't know that."

"Well, why don't you show them?"

I didn't have a clue how to work my way back into my children's lives, so they could see I'd changed. And I wasn't sure how to be a father now that they were all grown up. At least Lynn and Rick were by then, Julie was a teenager and, for all I knew, she didn't even know I was her father. I'd enjoyed being a dad when my kids were little, but that was all play. I don't think I even taught my kids much about life; Linda did most of that. But grown-up children, I was way out of my league. Hell, Lynn and Rick saw firsthand what I did with adult children.

I shook my head and Katherine stared at me for a few seconds.

"Don't you give up on them," she said. "Whatever you do, don't give up on those kids of yours."

"I haven't given up. I just don't know how to change things."

I'd changed for good and hoped my kids would come to see that someday, but I didn't have the right to ask anything from them: to give me another chance or even stay in touch with me. But I still didn't want to give up. I might not be like a father to them ever again, hadn't been one for decades, but I wanted some kind of relationship. Just didn't know how to get there.

My plan was to call every once in a while and check in with all my kids, but for some reason, I could never pick up that phone. Katherine always reminded me to call on their birthdays, but most years I'd let those days come and go without calling. I had all kinds of reasons for not calling, none of them any good. Didn't know what to say. Couldn't hear good over the phone anymore. It was too late in the day. I'll call tomorrow. On and on. As time passed, I felt bad and that made it harder to think about calling next time. It was a vicious circle.

CHAPTER 31
GHOSTS

Shortly after I walked away from the smuggling, I got an invitation to my thirtieth high-school reunion. I hadn't thought about my high-school buddies in decades but was really curious, and a little nostalgic, about what happened in their lives, what they became, where they'd gone. Only I didn't want them to know what I'd become, not the worst parts.

At the reunion, all the students' senior photos were on a poster board. Many of the pictures had a current photo next to it, so you could tell who was who, since we were all now a bunch of old farts. Next to my high-school photo was a blank spot, since I hadn't been in touch with anyone from this town for the past thirty years. I scanned the photos for my old friends Tom and Jay. Obviously older and much heavier, I hardly recognized the recent photo of Jay, but Tom hadn't changed much. His hair was graying and his face had a few wrinkles.

When I filled my old friends in on my life, I left out the details of about fifteen years. Those guys never went far from that little town, so they were pretty excited to hear about my days as an undercover narc in Miami. They'd all watched *Miami Vice* and couldn't believe I actually lived that life. The real Miami vice, they said, shaking their heads in astonishment.

The next day, Jay and Tom insisted on taking me for a drive. I recognized most of the town, but as we headed out of town, I lost my bearings until I saw a familiar street sign. Then I knew right where we were.

As we neared the old two-story farmhouse where I grew up, my throat tightened. We pulled into the driveway, and I stared at the rusted basketball hoop that still dangled from the shed. My father put that hoop up for me. I couldn't believe it was still there. That hoop flooded me with memories: shooting hoops out there every day, smoking cigarettes behind the shed, girls driving by and waving while we stood there holding our basketballs, waving back, hopeful.

When I walked up the front stairs, I remembered tiptoeing down those stairs as a teenager when I snuck out at night. The owners let me walk through the house. There were ghosts in those rooms, and one of them was me as a young man. I'd been so eager to start out on life, had every intention of following a straight and narrow path: Marine Corps, worshipping God, someday having a wife and kids. There I stood in the very room where I proposed to Linda. And that led to my first two children being born. And for a brief time, I stayed on that path, had a family and life was good. I did love my family, I truly did. Standing in my old house, I was fully aware of having lost a large part of my life.

Hanging out with smugglers isn't the same as being

with friends and family, because everything's focused on the cocaine and the money. That's all you think about and talk about and plan for. There isn't anything real in any of that. Smuggling is like being in the belly of an underworld and everyone's going on about life up in the sunshine, and you're stuck down in that dark place hiding and lying and scheming and scamming until you can't even remember what the light of day looks like.

The longer I stayed away from the smuggling life, the more I remembered what normal life was like and the closer and closer I came to my old self again. It was like I was circling back to the person I'd been all those years ago.

Katherine and I started going to my high-school reunion every year, and I became friends again with Jay and Tom. We had a lot of laughs together. Once Tom even called *me* for some career advice. If he only knew.

Me and Katherine also started getting together with her family, having them over for holidays, things that normal families did. These were so simple, but were things I hadn't done in years. Including things like getting a job. A real job.

You think I would've had a lot of that drug money left and wouldn't need to work, but I pissed so much of it away. Always told myself I'd invest some of that money in a legit business—not like the auction company, a really lucrative business that would make money—but I never did. Some of the money I put to good use. Bought houses and condos for me and my folks, bought some nice cars and trucks over the years. But after we paid off my hospital bills, there wasn't much left.

The first time I walked back into the auction house, I knew I had to let that business go. The association between that place and my old life was powerful, my palms got sweaty just walking through the front doors. I visualized all the places I stashed coke in that building, which got me pondering if I'd forgotten a few kilos tucked away somewhere. Hell, some cocaine could still be stashed in that building. Wouldn't that be funny if an electrician was working on the wiring and discovered a quarter-kilo of Colombian in the ceiling? That'd be one lucky bastard. Or maybe a very happy family of mice are running around in circles up in the ceiling with their little hearts racing. My stomach gurgled with excitement just thinking about tipping that ceiling panel up to check for any old stash. I sold my share in the company within a few months of getting out of the hospital.

With the profit from the auction barn, Katherine and I purchased a country store and Hickory Ham franchise. I was on a mission to replace that old lifestyle with some good, clean living. And a decent income. That store didn't exactly have us rolling in cash, despite working six days a week, and the work became boring pretty quickly—the highlight was the mad rush we had for whole hams during the holidays. Whoopee.

We did have one very exciting day in the country store. A few months after opening the store, I looked up from the deli counter when the front bells rattled. I knew instantly who the middle-aged woman was, despite her hair now being blonde. It was Laura. Which meant the teenaged girl behind her was Julie.

Laura's face was expressionless. "Hi John. Do you have some time to talk?"

I tried to keep my jaw relaxed as I looked at her. No

point bringing up my money and emeralds, the stuff she cleared out of our bank account when I was in prison. It was long gone.

I smiled at Julie. "Sure. Sure I do. Let's go talk at a table in the back."

Laura hesitated. "Well, if you have some time to talk with Julie now, I'll just come back later. Let you two visit."

"Sure, I've got time," I said, glancing at Katherine.

Katherine nodded and took over the sandwiches I was working on.

"I'll be back in a few hours, okay, honey?" Laura gave Julie a quick hug. Julie rolled her eyes.

I motioned for Julie to follow me to a table in the back. "It sure is good to see you. You've grown into a pretty young lady."

Julie gave me a nervous little smile. "I wanted to … see you … to meet you."

Katherine brought us chips, soda and two hoagies piled with all the toppings. She slid the plates across the table. "Hey there," she said to Julie.

"This is my wife, Katherine," I said.

Julie looked confused, maybe not thinking that I'd be remarried. She gave Katherine a little wave. "Hey."

"It's nice to finally meet you. I knew who you were when you walked in the door. You look a lot like your half-sister, Lynn," Katherine said.

Julie looked over at me. "Really?"

I nodded. "But she's got green eyes."

"You look the same as in the pictures I have of you," Julie said. I realized then she probably didn't remember me at all. She was barely five when I went to prison.

When Laura returned three hours later, Julie's eyes filled with tears. I told her she could come and stay with me and Katherine anytime.

"We'll see," Laura said. "Let me think about it and talk with Julie's father—"

"Step-father," Julie said.

I wasn't sure she'd let Julie see me again, but there was no point arguing with her; she had custody. I scribbled my phone number and address on a piece of paper and handed it to Laura. "Okay. Just say the word. We can come get her or whatever works. She's more than welcome at our house."

Julie and I did start seeing each other a couple times a year. And I started having more communication with Lynn and Rick too. That was still uncomfortable with all that unspoken stuff between us. Rick still lived in the same town, so I saw him the most. He'd stop by or call, tell me how his kids were doing, invite me to ball games or birthday parties.

Lynn started calling every once in a while, and it was always good to hear from her. But I didn't want to subject her to calls from me that she probably didn't want. When my father died, she came for the memorial. So did Rick and his family. Afterwards, I had everyone over for a barbecue. It made me happy to see both my kids doing so well. Somehow, they survived me.

I wrote Lynn a letter after that visit, basically apologizing for not being a great father. She wrote me right back and told me she no longer trusted me and forgiving me wasn't going to be that easy. As hard as it was for me to read those words, how could I blame her?

After that letter, I didn't have a clue how to work my way back into Lynn's life. Katherine suggested we stop by and visit her after my next high school reunion. So, I called to see if she'd be interested in a visit.

"We'll be passin' through next month, and I'd love to see you," I said. "Goin' to my high school reunion."

"Your reunion?" Lynn said. "You didn't even graduate from high school."

"I know, but I've been goin' every year. Lotta my old buddies are still around, and I like to see 'em every year. Can you believe they still remembered me?"

"Yeah, Dad. I believe it."

"What d'you say? Katherine and I'll buy you lunch."

Silence for several seconds. "Okay. Weekends are best. I've got classes during the week."

"Great. I'll call when we know the exact date. You can bring what's-his-name, that guy you're dating."

"I'm not seeing Rob anymore. It'll just be me."

We had lunch at a restaurant in a huge shopping mall in downtown Columbus. Lynn and Katherine gabbed up a storm, I chatted about my reunion and Lynn told us about her classes. She seemed to be watching me, assessing me, but that was okay. I didn't have anything to hide.

After lunch, Katherine wanted to check out the mall. While she went in and out of stores, Lynn and I sat on the benches in the middle of the mall and talked. Katherine would come out of one shop empty-handed, and I'd say, "Didn't find anything? Well, go on to the next store, darlin'."

I told Lynn about our country store. "It feels good to be working for real now. You know, a legitimate business."

She listened, nodded a bit, probably didn't believe me. I had a lot of "jobs" over the past fifteen years.

Katherine finally found a blouse and pair of jeans. "This mall is terrific," she said. "Nothing like this at home."

"That's for sure," I said. "Lynn, you need any—"

"No, I'm fine. Thanks."

"How 'bout one of those Cinnabons over there? I'm gonna look into a franchise. We don't have those in North Carolina yet. The way that cinnamon smell fills up the mall, they must make a killin'."

Katherine and Lynn looked at each other and laughed.

"What? I bet they do."

Lynn shook her head. "It's just funny. How you're just always trying to make a killing."

"Nothin' wrong with that."

"Depends on how you're trying to do it," Katherine said.

"Exactly why I wanna go check out those cinnamon rolls."

Those *were* really good cinnamon rolls. And I looked into a franchise; way too expensive. But that visit with Lynn, that was a little turning point for us.

Slowly, over time, things got more comfortable with her. Things weren't great, but at least Lynn, Rick and Julie were still in my life. That was really all I could ask for. We had some kind of relationship. As good as a Walker relationship could be.

CHAPTER 32
MAKIN' A KILLIN'

W e eventually sold that country store, Katherine went back to work and graduate school to become a school counselor, and I got a series of different jobs. I worked in a hospital cafeteria, a high-school kitchen, even drove a bus for a private school. Course, I lied on those job applications about my felonies. Guess they didn't check federal records.

Lucky for me, jobs, what I did or the security of them, just weren't that important to me. I figured if I left a job or a paycheck today, I'd make it up tomorrow. Like all that drug money that came and went, everything in life does that—jobs, money, health, relationships. Having lived that high-rolling life, cash stuffed everywhere, made money less important to me. I'd had it all and lost it all, and I was still standing.

The jobs I liked most were ones that involved selling stuff. Selling was probably the closest I could get to experiencing that game. Suppose I always loved that. Probably why I was such a good smuggler: I was just selling my product. Came in handy as an undercover agent too, when I was "selling" dealers that I was one of them. I could still talk to anyone about anything, only now what I was talking about was real stuff. I wasn't fooling people about who I was, trying to remember my lies or looking over my shoulder whispering about drugs.

I usually had at least a side job selling things at flea markets or shows: costume jewelry, knife sharpeners, men's clothing. My favorite was a hot-dog stand I had in the parking lot of the hardware store. Course, there's no comparison, money- or thrill-wise, between selling Colombian cocaine and hot dogs.

Rick helped me with the hot-dog stand, off and on, and I gave him half the profit. Figured he could use the extra cash, and I sure needed the help. By the time I loaded the fuel tanks, coolers full of product and hitched the trailer with the grill to my truck, I'd have to stop and catch my breath. I was getting too old for this shit, but, man, did it feel good to be out there meeting people, chatting and laughing, talking up my product. When I drop dead, I hope I'm doing something exciting, not laying around in a hospital bed. Or like my father, sitting around for years tatting—whatever the hell that is—tablecloths. Much rather go out with a bang than a dribble.

As I drove to our meeting location, I calculated how much we could make, how much money I'd spent already and how I could increase my profit. It all depended on the location. I needed to find the right spot where there were plenty of buyers.

Rick and I unloaded the truck and had everything all set up when here came our first potential customers: a middle-aged man and his wife. She wasn't half-bad looking.

"Afternoon. How y'all doin'? Please tell me you're not takin' that lovely lady into the hardware store on an empty stomach." She smiled at me. I had them. I pointed at the dogs, plump and perfectly browned on my grill. "These are the *best* hot dogs you're ever gonna eat. However you like 'em, I got it. 'Kraut. Chili. Onions. Relish. Four kinds of mustard. You name it, I got it. Give you two for ten. If it's not the best dog you've ever tried, I'll refund your money on the way back out."

The lady looked expectantly at her husband. My first sale of the day. The man pulled out his wallet while the woman smiled at me again

Oh yeah, we're gonna make a killin' today.

###

EPILOGUE: A BEGINNING

I t's been a year since my first interview with Dad, and he just read a draft of this story. He taps the stack of pages on the coffee table between us. "Man, I had no idea you could write like this. You captured everything I told you: all the action and thrill of police work, the smuggling and easy money, the cocaine highs and lows, all of it. This is really good stuff. You oughta turn this into a book."

"You want me to try to publish your story?"

He nods.

"Really? You'd support that?"

"Sure. Why not?"

"I was worried it would be … I don't know … too difficult for you to read. That you'd just bury it in a drawer or something."

"Oh, there's some stuff in there I thought I'd take to the grave. But since you're my daughter, I suppose it's your legacy—good and bad." He pauses for a moment. "Sure wish there'd been more good to tell you about. Least I hope you got your questions answered, that all this helped you somehow."

"It definitely helped. Because … well … because I finally got to know you."

Dad holds my gaze for a long moment. In that empty space between us, I'm comfortable, finally, with silence.

"Been kind of a long way to get to know your father, huh?"

I give a shrug. "Yeah. A little." I always went easy on Dad, even when I shouldn't have.

"Well … if that's all that comes from this, I'd say we did pretty good then."

AFTERWORD BY THE AUTHOR

To my knowledge, my father never smuggled again. When he died at age 72, Katherine gave me some of his belongings, including a photograph of me as a teenager. I hadn't seen that photo in decades. She found it in an envelope in his file cabinet. As I looked at my fourteen-year-old self, smiling for the camera, which was held by my then-boyfriend and drug dealer, I was bowled over with compassion for my younger self. It was a turbulent, self-destructive time that I, somehow, survived.

But how had my father gotten the photo?

Then my finger grazed a tiny rough spot on the back. Flipping it over, I saw a small pinhole in the top of the photo, so small that it wasn't noticeable from the front. I worried my fingertip back and forth over that little tag, trying to figure out how he got a photo of me. Especially since Dad was in prison by then.

That was it! This was the photo I'd sent, along with a letter, when he was in prison. And then he'd kept it, somehow carried it with him, for another thirty years.

The realization made that old feeling flicker in me, that feeling of hope that I had carried for so many decades. Even with Dad now gone, I was still thrilled at any hint, any proof, that he loved me. I smiled slightly at the tenacity of that feeling. The small ripple of hope washed back out to sea, not pulling me with it this time. Not anymore.

I imagined—no, I was certain—the pinhole was from where my father had tacked the picture to his prison wall all those years. As I held that photo of myself, I wondered if he ever looked at my smiling face and if *he* felt hope. Or maybe he stood there in his prison cubicle, stared at my face and felt joy, maybe chuckled at a memory of me as a child. Maybe somedays, he looked at that photo of me and felt love.

I hope so.

Dad just out of prison & up for my high school graduation.

ALSO BY LYNN WALKER

Midnight Calling: A Memoir of a Drug Smuggler's Daughter

Follow Lynn Walker for news of her next book:

www.LynnWalkerMemoir.com

social media: @WalkerMemoir

THANKS FOR THE READ!

If you feel inspired to do so, please tell a friend about this book and post a review on Amazon, Goodreads or your favorite online bookstore.

Made in the USA
Middletown, DE
16 May 2023

30664092R00179